Vitality in Everyday Life

with inspiration from Ayurveda

Eva Forsberg Schinkler

Vitality in Everyday Life

with inspiration from Ayurveda

Previous editions

First edition Livskraft i vardagen med inspiration av Ayurveda
(Norstedts, 2009)

The Art of Eating – eller konsten att äta med inspiration av
Ayurveda (Blad by Blad, 2011)

© 2009, 2015, 2017, 2020 Eva Forsberg Schinkler

Photo: Dan Ljungsvik and Evalena Andersson
Design cover: Helene Hansson

Publisher: BoD – Books on Demand, Stockholm, Sweden
Print: BoD – Books on Demand, Norderstedt, Germany

ISBN: 9789178512607

To my children Viktor and Maria

and to my soulmate Philip

Contents

Introduction

Many years ago, while at university, I wrote an essay about the healing ability of mankind and I realised that something was missing. Something fundamental about why human beings differ from each other, and why we thrive on different things, which at that point I had not yet understood. Some people thrive on stress, tight deadlines and challenges. Others shun pressure and challenges like the plague and would rather take it nice and easy and keep things the way they are. Eventually, curiosity got the better of me. What exactly is it that controls and initiates healing in us? Apparently, it varies quite a lot, so I started searching for something that could describe and make me understand this complex system.

The questions I asked myself and which have since accompanied me on my life journey, are:

1. What makes us healthy?
2. What gives us vitality and makes us positive?
3. What is it that makes some people better than others at turning adversity into prosperity?

At that time, about a dozen years ago, when stress and burnout was a hot topic, I discovered Ayurveda. After having studied human physiology, psychology and behaviour, I realized that Ayurveda was exactly what I was looking for. Ayurveda describes precisely the complexity surrounding human healing, not only our ability to free ourselves of discomfort and disease, but also what we can do to feel really well and have vitality and a zest for life in our everyday lives. Ayurveda is a simple way of describing something that is fairly complex, but since it is easy to explain, each of us can apply its basic principles to improve all aspects of our lives. By following the principles of Ayurveda you will enhance your understanding of yourself and what is behind your good and bad habits, and above all, understand what it is you need to feel good. You will learn what the driving force is in your work and which talents and strengths you should develop to achieve your goals. You will also gain an insight into how you can boost your self-healing abilities and live a healthier life. Ayurveda is a great complement to other approaches, is dogma free and does not describe how things should be. Rather, it is a way of understanding how everything affects us. If you understand what affects you and how people around you are affected by you, you can also begin to move towards that which makes you healthier, more vibrant, and gives you vitality in everyday life.

This book is intended as a practical book to inspire you, in which you will find practical tips on attaining more power, pleasure and well-being in your everyday life. Each chapter will bring you one step further into the world of Ayurveda and each chapter is followed by a section of tips for you to try right away. However, this is not a traditional Ayurveda book. I have been inspired by various traditions, both through modern research and knowledge I have gained from meetings with shamans and medicine men and women, all from different cultures, who all affirm essentially the same knowledge. I found the description of Ayurveda straightforward and thus the easiest to understand. Therefore, I apply the knowledge I have gained in most of what I do today, from guiding people to better lifestyles to coaching managers in large organizations.

This book will give you the opportunity to take a self-test to establish which Ayurveda personality type you are. It is not a means to an end, it is simply a stepping stone to better understand what it is you are doing well and where you can grow in order to create balance.

Ayurveda has been known in the West for a long time and the World Health Organization (WHO) has endorsed the principles of Ayurveda since the seventies, considering Ayurveda one of the most effective ways to approach public health in the Third World. It is inexpensive and suitable for treatment that you can implement yourself. It is worth noting that several athletes apply the principles of Ayurveda to enhance their performance and stamina. So, consider what you would like to achieve by reading this book. Ask yourself the following questions: How good do I want to feel right now? How good do I want to feel in ten years?

The following short story is food for thought to keep in mind while reading this book.

A professor stood in front of his philosophy class with a few items in front of him. As the class began, he quietly picked up a very large, empty glass jar and began filling it to the brim with golf balls. He then asked the students if the jar was full. They agreed it was.

The professor then picked up a box of pebbles and poured them into the jar.
He shook the jar lightly. The pebbles rolled into the space between the golf balls. Again, he asked the students if the jar was full? They agreed it was.

Next, the professor picked up a box of sand and poured it into the jar. The sand filled up the left-over space. He asked, once more, if the jar was full. The students responded unanimously: "Yes".

Then, the professor produced two cups of coffee from under the table and poured the contents into the jar, effectively filling the empty space between the sand.

The students laughed.

Now, said the professor as the laughter subsided, I want you to perceive this jar as your life.

The golf balls are the important things, such as family, children, health and anything else close to your heart. Things that, if everything else was lost and only they remained, your life would still be full.

The pebbles represent other things that matter, like your job and car. The sand is everything else – the small stuff. If you put

12

*the sand into the jar first, he continued, it is not possible to
make room for the pebbles or the golf balls. The same goes for
life. If you spend all your time and energy on the small stuff,
there will be no room left for what really matters to you. So, pay
attention to the things that are crucial to your happiness. Play
with your children. Take your partner out to dinner. Devote
more time to that which fills you with passion.*

*Sooner or later you can clean the house and do less important
things. Take care of the golf balls first – the things that really
matter. Address the most important things in your life. The rest
is just sand. One of the students raised her hand and asked what
the coffee represented. The professor smiled and said, I'm glad
you asked that. It just goes to show that however full your life
may seem, there is always room for coffee with a friend.*

I wish you a pleasant reading!

Stockholm, January 2020   Eva Forsberg Schinkler

1

Vitality and Ayurveda

"We tend to forget that happiness doesn't come as a result of getting something we don't have, but rather of recognizing and appreciating what we do have."

Frederick Koenig

We are all different, are we not?

For a long time, human beings have created systems trying to understand the order of the world. We have created classifications for flowers, animals, stars, molecules, yes for almost everything, except humans. Everyone is aware that we are all different, but how does it really work? Could it be coincidence, along with heritage and environment, that makes us who we are? Probably, but certain differences remain, based on which we can actually create patterns to gain a better understanding of ourselves. Have you ever wondered why some people seem to be able to eat as much as they like without gaining weight, while others just need to take one look at food to put on a few kilos? Or why some people come over as quick and witty while others are calmer and more stable? Some people walk fast while others move slowly. Some people talk fast and spontaneously while others are reflective and thoughtful. Well, these differences are not coincidences. They did not happen randomly, indeed a system explaining our differences has already been developed. Ayurveda is an ancient, unique system that describes our differences in an easy and understandable way, which helps us appreciate that we need different things at different times in our lives, in order to keep our life vitality in balance.

Ayurveda has been described as a very old and experienced-based knowledge. The origin of this philosophy is in the Veda culture, founded on the Indian continent and believed to be over 10,000 years old. Ayurveda was conceived about 3,000 to 5,000 years ago and the philosophy is said to illustrate how to live in harmony and balance. "Ayur" means life and "Veda" means knowledge, in Sanskrit, an ancient language which was spoken on the Indian subcontinent during this period. I have translated Ayurveda to "The Knowledge of Life" or better still, to "Everyday Knowledge", as the principles offers a comprehensible and effortless way to live a more harmonious life and allow us to build on our strengths. Ayurveda provides contemporary people with a foundation for taking more responsibility for our own health and well-being, that does not involve any dos and don'ts.

Although Ayurveda is a fairly complex system, the principles are reasonably easy to understand, which makes the system easy to use.

Most cultures, even Western culture, have theories for the existence of everything from the universe to the mountains, from human beings to small molecules, which make use of five elements. Physics have defined them as: vacuum, gas, energy, liquid and solid. Physics explains density, or the distance between molecules and atoms. The distance between gas molecules is so vast the gas is not visible to the naked eye, although we can feel the air we breathe, for example. We discern the effect of energy when the heat of a fire reaches us. Liquid molecules have gathered together close enough that we can see them and there is no doubt that the chair we are sitting on is a mass structure, for instance.

However, ancient cultures had already adopted similar theories. Native Indians of North and South America talk about the Medicine Wheel comprising the four elements of Earth, Wind, Fire and Water, with the fifth element, Space, in the centre. Many native cultures have explained the structure of the universe similarly, from the Sami people in Scandinavia to the Aborigines in Australia and the Maoris in the South Pacific, to name a few.

The quantum physics model describes everything as vibration, even the atoms and molecules that make up our physical body. Human DNA vibrates at a frequency of 52-78 gigahertz (billions of cycles per second). This is worth considering while quietly and peacefully meditating! It would not be out of place to say that all human beings have their own personal, unique vibration. We often refer to energy when we meet other people. Some exude positive and life-giving energy, others calm and peaceful energy and we have all met someone who saps our energy; energy drainers. We can clearly feel when our power and energy is high, or when we feel empty and powerless. Basically, we are all energy-vibrating beings with our own natural rhythms. Ayurvedic philosophy provides an understanding of these rhythms and how they affect us all throughout our lives. Consequently, you can boost your self-awareness as well as your understanding of other people, which will help you make more well-informed, day-to-day choices and consequently ultimately improve how you feel, give you more vitality and, above all, give you the power and energy to achieve exactly what you want in life.

The Medicine Wheel

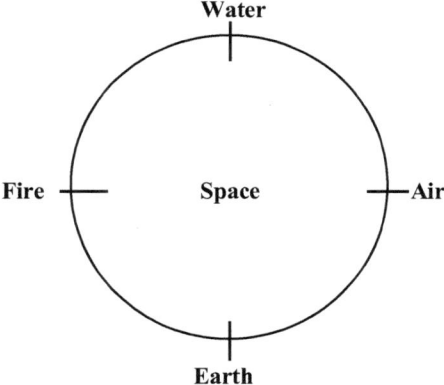

The model above is showing the five elements: Space, Air, Fire, Water and Earth. As you can see yhey can be defined in physics terms as Space = Vacuum, Air = Gas, Fire = Energy, Water = Liquid and Earth = Mass; and you will also see that they are, similar to in the western world, used in the same context to explain the elements. Calling the elements by the slightly more poetic terms Space, Air, Fire, Water and Earth I feel provides a closer insight into the characteristics of each element. Space is light, empty and hollow; Air is light, volatile and changeable; Fire is warm, hot and burning; Water is rich, moist and clean; while Earth is compact, quiet and stable. Just as everything around us is made up of these five elements in different arrangements, so are all human beings. What is unique to Ayurveda is that the ayurvedic philosophy drew attention to the fact that the five elements form the foundation for three different energies, which can be found in everything and in Sanskrit are called Vata, Pitta and Kapha. Vata means wind and the element symbolising motion, lightness, hollowness and change. Pitta means fire and symbolises, burning, heating, melting and penetration. Kapha symbolises reinforcement, lubrication and cohesion.

Vata = space + air

Pitta = fire + a little water

Kapha = earth + water

According to the ayurvedic tradition, all of the five elements of Space, Air, Fire, Water and Earth, and therefore also the three energies of Vata, Pitta and Kapha, can be found in everything. Together the three energies, or doshas (the traditional name for the energies), govern all life processes. Vata regulates the catabolic processes, Pitta regulates transformation, and Kapha regulates the anabolic processes. By understanding what the characteristics of Vata, Pitta and Kapha entail, we can begin to understand the processes at work, irrespective of what we are studying: the weather, economy, animals, food or people. The trick is to know which energy is dominant, which will then give us an understanding of what is going on and how to balance the process.

Features and functions of the three energies, Vata, Pitta and Kapha

Dosha Functions Features

Vata (Space and Air). Regulates any processes associated with movement and decay.

Variable

Quick, fast

Light

Dry

Rough

Clear

Cold

Controls the other two doshas since movement is always required for something to happen.

Pitta (fire and water). Represent the functions associated with warmth, burning and transformation.

Hot

Sharp

Easy

Penetrating

Sour

Slightly oily

Kapha (earth and water). Represent lubrication, reinforcement and cohesion.

Solid

Heavy

Oily

Cold

Sweet

Sticky

Slow

Soft

Once you have gained a better understanding of these concepts, you will begin to see what you are being dominated and influenced by, and whether the influences stem from the mind, work, weather, economic trends, friends, etc.

Explaining health and illness is a complex issue. Ever since Western medicine was established centuries ago, man has endeavoured to find a different cause for each disease. Now, we are beginning to grasp that health and illness involve a multitude of events that cannot be explained by simple answers such as, lack of, or excess of, any substance. There will always be another question to ask: Why? The philosophy of Ayurveda is based on the understanding that *everything* affects us. EVERYTHING! The only question is: How? Supported by our comprehension of the three energies, Vata, Pitta and Kapha, as well as the qualities they are dominated by, Ayurveda has, since time immemorial, been a way of understanding how we are affected by various things and events, and that each individual is affected differently. You might like being busy, to live an active life with plenty of interests, eat hot cooked meals, take really hot baths or enjoy some peace and quiet, while other people prefer the complete opposite.

It is interesting to compare Ayurveda to other medical doctrines as to how and why it is believed people differ. For instance, research into behavioural medicine is also showing a system based on our differences. Studies have revealed that cardiovascular disease is overrepresented in people referred to as having Type A personalities. Type A personalities are considered stressed, interrupt often, are distinctly competitive and easily become irritated and aggressive. According to this research, hostility and cynicism are behind the increase in cardiovascular diseases. The same research sought to explain other behavioural traits that do not result in stress disorders and cardiovascular disease to the same extent. These traits are attributed to as Type B personalities, characterised by calmness, security and stability and a less competitive spirit. Type C personalities are overrepresented in chronic diseases such as cancer, although to date research is very limited. Presumably, the desire to comprehend what it is that keeps us healthy and what makes us ill, is inherent in human beings. In our culture, the main focus has been to understand what makes us sick, depressed and to lose our energy. Doctors have gathered data on ill people in a bid to understand what health is, psychologists have studied mental illness in order to understand what makes us happy, while teachers have mostly concentrated on our weaknesses in order to help us develop our strengths. These negative based strategies could not be more wrong! The understanding of what makes us healthy, happy and strong, to keep us from getting physically or mentally ill, is lacking. Ayurvedic knowledge provides us with opportunities to be more responsible for our own well-being. The principles do not only give us the means to live healthier lives, they also provide support for developing our strengths as well as guidance to help us live more harmoniously despite any external and internal pressures we are all faced with in life.

I have combined a number of different approaches to create conditions for healing and well-being. Understanding that each person is unique with their own innate combination of the three energies of Vata, Pitta and Kapha, will increase the understanding of our differences. Accepting that we all have different needs we have our own unique rhythm can be a real eye-opener and an insight to the fact that we are not odd or deviant because our needs differ from other people's needs. It is particularly satisfying to take on board the different needs and behaviours of those closest to you; your partner, your children, friends or colleagues.

When we understand of our own behavioural patterns, which skills and strengths we possess becomes clear. There is a particular method of identifying an individual's strengths and preconditions within Ayurveda, utilised by each individual to create well-being with the support of their surroundings. Everyone has strengths, even those who try their best to disguise theirs. Most people are aware of what is good and what is bad for them, and they also know how to solve their problems and achieve balance with good support and guidance. Gaining greater insight into ourselves based on Vata, Pitta and Kapha, we will better understand how to increase our vitality by compensating, enhancing and changing little things in our everyday lives.

To have vitality and zest for life are expressions for having flow in life, and the resources to see how we can achieve our goals as effortlessly as possible. This means that you can deal with stressful situations in life through strain rather than hardship. Stress can make you feel as though you are on a battleground or swimming upstream. We feel it when the demands of life outweigh our resources. Strain, on the other hand, has the opposite effect and supports us in our quest of reaching or even exceeding our goals through what many people describe as 'flow', rather than struggling through. One of the biggest obstacles to experiencing vitality and zest for life is the common conception that we do not have all the resources needed to be in flow. There is always something that we seem to lack; money, love, friends, things, jobs, self-reliance, confidence, energy, etc. You can probably bring out your own favourite obstacles as an effective way to prevent yourself from achieving your full potential.

Human beings have the ability to think negatively. We often fall into the pattern of seeing obstacles, problems and risks, even though we know that it is important to think positively and focus on the possibilities, solutions and joy to feel good and be successful. None of us has ever had to attend a "Learn to think negatively" course. This ability has been given to us for free, so to speak. So, you are in good company if you often react negatively to involuntary changes. This type of behaviour is an ancestral trait in most of us. We have simply been equipped with a negative filter through which we view the world as soon as we feel we may lose control. Since the beginning of humanity, our survival strategy has been based on threats and risks. What do you think would have happened if people ran happily out on to the savannah 50,000 years ago, without weighing up the risk of being eaten by a lion? Or what would have happened if a person entered a forest and ate the red mushrooms without considering the risk? Humanity, as we know it, would have been extinct a long time ago. Being able to calculate risks and threats in our everyday lives is actually advantageous. You should be grateful for that skill as it helps you survive! Problems arise if we get stuck in negative behavioural patterns revolving around risks and threats to our survival. Threats may include lack of money, too much work or no work at all, a bad relationship or the lack of a relationship, and so on. Learning to recognize our natural tendency to spiral into negativity in situations we cannot control, can help us understand: firstly, it is completely normal to view events negatively and, secondly, we need to train ourselves to see solutions, and opportunities and experience the joy of life. And it will come. Those who have gone before us will guide us. It is not about what we are doing, but how we handle different situations. It is evident that everyone has the capacity to change their ways and begin to view life from a different perspective. We will look into how further on.

Today, a new focus within established psychology called Positive Psychology is emerging. Finally, interest in finding out what makes us feel good is gaining momentum besides only focusing on what makes us feel broken and like losers. If we focus on happiness and well-being, these qualities tend to grow. We will always get more of that which we spend most of our energy and focus on. The American sociologist Aaron Antonovsky, who emigrated to Israel in the 1960s, carried out research on former Jewish concentration camp prisoners during the 1970s. His research revealed that people who have been exposed to terrible atrocities have the capacity to carry on and enjoy a good quality of life. The research was ground-breaking as it showed that concentration camp survivors that was enjoying a good quality of life afterwards, had not been exposed to less harrowing experiences than others. It became clear that they had adopted a coping strategy to handle the situation they found themselves in, to preserve their life vitality during this difficult time. Antonovsky found that these people had in common was that they felt Sense of Coherence, referred to as SOC. He identified three concepts in reference to SOC: 1) Comprehensibility - they could create an understanding of what happened and why; 2) Manageability - they had the capability to handle new circumstances in a crucial moment of their lives; 3) Meaningfulness - they found a meaning in continuing the struggle to survive, they created an inner world that gave them the objectives to understand the possibilities in their lives. Antonovsky's SOC theory, based on these three concepts, is still being used today to provide support to those wishing to develop themselves. Ponder the three concepts and how you describe your daily life.

1. **Comprehensibility**, *why* things are the way they are.
2. **Manageability**, *how* you handle everyday life.
3. **Meaningfulness**, *what* adds value in your life.

Eastern philosophy has a long tradition of practicing how to handle life as it is, a kind of acceptance and life satisfaction. Deepak Chopra, an Indian Doctor living in the US, explains that Eastern tradition teaches acceptance of life as it is, while traditionally in the West, we believe that we have capacity to influence almost everything and create our own existence. Both traditions pose a certain amount of risk. By keeping on accepting what life throws at you, you risk losing the energy you need to make changes to aspects of your life that does not serve you: poor self-esteem, poverty or even climate change, for example. The belief that we are our own God, trying to satisfy our needs, generally only with the means of external attributes, makes for disheartened people when happiness cannot be found in money or the things they own.

The next phase may give us the ability to combine these two approaches to allow us to be both productive in the external world while maintaining a deep-rooted meaningfulness inside ourselves. The majority of successful people who have profoundly served humanity on our planet have adopted this particular combination: Nelson Mandela, Mother Teresa, Martin Luther King and

Muhammad Yunus of Grameen Bank are just a few of those who have displayed these two characteristics. There are people around us who have the ability to connect deeply with their inner meaningfulness, and who have been able to develop this skill in their own lives. Maybe you are one of them. If not, let yourself be inspired by them. We all have the capacity to realize our inner selves through the external world. Had that not been the case mankind would have remained in the Stone Age. We all have unexplored skills that we might be unaware of, or have not been brave enough to expose. We often are more afraid of our strengths than our weaknesses. Imagine what could happen if we allowed ourselves to shine and take advantage of our full potential. However, people around us might feel inferior and even a failure. That is why we often stand back and avoid upsetting those close to us.

Finding the language to express ourselves can sometimes be the key to escaping this trap and start using our strengths and talents. Never has the need for our planet to produce fresh creative talents with the capacity to view things from a new perspective, been so apparent. A perspective where everything, people, animals and nature, can happily co-exist in harmony. Marshall Rosenberg the American psychologist who established Non-Violent Communication, a way of communicating peacefully has defined a communication method involving the heart as well as the brain. He mentions a particularly important issue which he calls "slave language," a type of language we frequently adopt. Slave language include words like *shall, should, ought to,* words that do not allow us to make our own choices. When we constantly say "must" to ourselves, or to others for that matter, the most primitive part of ourselves asserts itself. Be prepared for trouble if you say "must" to a four-year old child. Nobody likes to feel forced by themselves or by anyone else. Instead, start using words that simplify your life. Try replacing the words "must", "should" and "ought to" with "need", a word that allows you to feel that you have a choice.

In order to make changes, we must first become aware of what we would like to change. Usually, it is only when something in life is physically, mentally or spiritually uncomfortable, when it gets really bad, that we begin looking for ways of making changes. Which is a good starting point. Then we need to gain an insight into what to do to achieve a positive outcome. At this point it is important to keep practicing, or they will remain empty words. There are many ways to reach healing, health and vitality: you just go out and try. The ayurvedic way of describing a complex reality can provide you with simple tools that you start using in your everyday life. Begin by establishing what you would like to improve. Some of us are already smart enough and do not wait until something goes wrong, we continuously find ways to improve ourselves, to feel even better. Ayurveda will show you how to make best use of your strengths and talents. We all have the constitutions we were born with. This book will help you realize that it is perfectly possible to create a successful life based on your unique circumstances. You are perfect just the way you are!

You will find out more in the next chapter about the ayurvedic description of Vata, Pitta and Kapha in different situations. Simply identify which of the different descriptions suits you best. Like most people you will probably find that your personality traits span two of the three doshas. By identifying which apply most to you and any potential imbalances you may have, you will be guided to what you can focus on, to create balance. As you have probably realized by now, features from all the doshas are found in each of us, but some of the characteristics will dominate your personality more than others. When you start understanding more about yourself and your habits in different situations, you will easily grasp what you need to balance to increase your vitality.

Coaching tips:

- *What is most important in your life? Prioritize.*
- *What creates context in your life; Work? Family? Friends? Health and Well-being? Time for reflection? You can ask yourself, what would happen if you should lose any of the things you just mentioned?*
- *What do you want more of in your life?*
- *What do you want less of, or simply delete from your life, if you receive more of what you mentioned above?*
- *Finally, how willing are you to change, to create what you really want to achieve?*

2

Our differences

"Be yourself; everyone else is already taken."

Oscar Wilde

On my journey through life, I developed an understanding of the differences that I realised early on exist between us. Despite having been born into the same family, served the same food at home and having many things in common, our personalities and habits can still be polar opposites. Eventually, what initially appeared to me as an interesting observation, became an integral part of my philosophy of life. It gave me the insight that I am in charge of my life, and as such I am actively able to choose a life focusing on strength and energy - enhancing activities and reject anything that saps my strength and energy. You too can do the same. First, you have to understand which personality type you are dominated by. Next, look at what brings your personality type in balance and off balance. Lastly, you actively have to choose what creates balance and increased vitality in your life, and reject anything that drains your energy. It is your decision! The only thing you risk by following the tips and advice in this book, is that your life may improve.

So, the first thing to do when looking for ways to self-heal and boost well-being, is to start by considering your everyday habits. We have usually picked up our habits by watching our parents as we were growing up. However, it is becoming increasingly evident that contemporary habits are not in tune with how humans were created to live. As soon as we become aware of our habits we start noticing that our preferences may be different to the preferences of other people. Some are morning people and wake up by themselves early in the morning, while others are night owls and like to stay awake late into the night. Some delight in pushing themselves towards a target while others prefer a slower rhythm. Before addressing somebody's symptoms or imbalances, ayurvedic tradition looks into who the person is. Initially we must establish what personality type we are, both physically and mentally, based on the Vata, Pitta and Kapha constitutions. Then we need to answer the question of why any discomfort or imbalance has arisen. We begin by looking at the different elements (space, air, fire, water and earth) in the shape of the three different qualities Vata, Pitta and Kapha that exist within us all.

The three energies are present in all human beings because everything is made up of a combination of the five elements and therefore, also of Vata, Pitta and Kapha. The question is which quality, or dosha as they are called, we are dominated by both physically and psychologically. When we analyse ourselves, we will realise that most of us are dominated in our unique way by one, or most commonly two, of these doshas. One dosha is not better than another and the combination present in you, is unique to you.

When you continue to read about Vata, Pitta and Kapha, you will understand that a combination of the different characteristics each of the three energies represent, exists in us all. You are never one or the other, always a combination. It is not an end in itself to establish your personality type. The aim is to provide you with advice, based on your unique needs, if you should want to create more vitality in your life by improving your physical, mental and spiritual well-being. Since we are all different, our needs for achieving good health differ too. Aided by ayurvedic tradition, you will gain a better understanding of yourself and become more alert to how you feel. Ayurveda will also guide you to simple ways of helping yourself. I had the opportunity to closely watch the work of ayurvedic doctors while in-house training at an ayurvedic clinic for the destitute in India. Before exploring any imbalances, ayurvedic practice requires an initial understanding of which personality type dominates a patient, followed by guidance, recommendations and treatment, based on the principles of how to balance any imbalances that have arisen in the doshas. It was fascinating watching the Ayurveda doctors, who have acquired considerable knowledge of the various qualities of Vata, Pitta and Kapha. They were incredibly fast at gathering substantial amounts of information about a patient by using their five senses, whereas our doctors would rely more on various measuring instruments. Many patients had already visited doctors who had trained in modern medicine for various tests or X-rays. They then visited the ayurvedic doctor who, within minutes, came to the same conclusion as the test results they had brought, before even looking at the test results! Several medically trained observers attended the clinic and we were all astounded at the level of accuracy in their expert opinion. I am optimistically anticipating future developments whereby left-brained knowledge in the West can be integrated with right-brained knowledge in the East. It is evident that knowledge beyond our modern thinking exists, which would be useful for us to understand and apply if we want to improve our well-being to 100 %.

Below is a simplified self-assessment test of the three doshas. Read each statement and write 1 in front of the statement that best describes you. If you find that two statements apply equally, write 0.5 by each. Once done, add up each column and add your score to the boxes at the bottom. Now you will see which dosha scores the highest, comes second, and which scores the least. Most likely you, like most people, will have two doshas dominating your personality. As you have probably already realised, this is a simplified way of finding out your personality type, which may serve as a wake-up call to start thinking about doing things differently in your everyday life. It is not until we become aware of something, that we can do something about it. You will also discover that should you repeat the test after reading the entire book, your results might be different, because you will then have gained a greater understanding of yourself and your answers may also be more honest. The interesting thing is that, relatively quickly, you will begin to see how other people are and behave, while your own patterns are not always easy to recognise. Therefore, make use of your friends and ask them how they perceive you.

When you try to find your own profile, focus on the features you recognize. There is nothing that says we are either one or the other. The point being that you should get a better understanding of why you spontaneously act in a certain way. If you feel good, feel harmony and in balance, from the ayurvedic perspective it means that you are living in harmony with your personality profile, where you make smart, everyday choices that create your balance. Most of us know deep down what we need, to feel good.

The Test

Simplified Ayurveda Personality Profile

The different energies of Vata, movement, Pitta, heat and Kapha, supportive, rule all functions both physical and psychological and exist in everyone. You have different characteristic depending on the extent to which the different energies dominate. The questions below are a simplified version of an Ayurveda test, to give you a rough idea about your personality profile.

	Vata	**Pitta**	**Kapha**
Bone structure	Thin	Medium	Heavy
Weight	Low, weight gain difficult	Medium weight	High, weight gain easy
Endurance	Low	Medium	High

Movement	Quick and easy	Determined and fast	Slow and calm
Work	Very fast	Efficiently and conscientiously	Slow and methodically
Mental function	Imaginative, quick-witted, decision making difficult	Sharp intellect, decision making easy	Stable, needs time for reflection
New ideas	Inquisitive, like trying new things	Investigate critical, before adopting new ideas	Prefer to wait, not impulsive
Mood	Changeable	Temperamental	Stable
Stress response	Excitable, anxious	Irritable, angry, fault-finding, judging	Rarely irritable or anxious but closed and silent
Skin	Dry, easily tanned, less subcutaneous fat	Sensitive, easily burned	Smooth, soft, sometimes greasy
Sleep	Easily woken, early riser	Regular sleeping habits, likes sleeping 8 hrs/night	Heavy sleep and tired in the morning

Hunger and metabolism	Irregular, sometimes forgets to eat	Very hungry, 'has to' eat	No clear hunger signals, can wait if necessary
Finances	Irresponsible, impulse purchases	Buys necessary things, good quality/often food and drink	Rarely impulsive purchases, prefer to save for the future
Total			

Vata controls all bodily movements

Vata represents the energy of movement, or flow, and all cavities in the body. Processes where movement is present include breathing, eye blinking, the movement of food through the body (peristalsis), the flow of blood through the body and the movement of the heart, the beating of the heart pushing blood throughout the body. Vata also controls the nervous system and our ability to use our five senses; sound, sight, touch, taste and smell, as Vata is responsible for the movement that allows neurons to communicate with each other. Our skeleton is dominated by Vata due to its tiny cavities. Vata is also involved in the decomposition process in the body.

Mentally, Vata stands for movement of the mind including creativity, flexibility, changeability, openness, sociability, activity and speed of thought.

Pitta controls metabolism and transformation of the body

Pitta regulates digestion and our ability to metabolize and decompose the food we eat, as well as our ability to feel hunger and thirst. It is Pitta that is in charge of metabolism and keeping the body warm. Blood is also represented by Pitta which provides nourishment to the entire body and skin. Skin, muscle and cell division are also part of the processes involved in digestion and transformation. Primarily, Pitta regulates our ability to ingest, convert and metabolise food in order to generate new tissue and energy.

Mentally, Pitta affects our ability to collect and digest external impressions, what we see, hear, feel, taste and smell. Cognitively, Pitta is also in charge of aspects of evaluation such as staying focused, critical, analytical, outgoing, determined, dedicated and controlled.

Kapha regulates reinforcement and lubrication in the body

Kapha governs mucus production and the mucous membranes to ensure that the moisture balance is correct in the body. Fatty tissue is governed by Kapha and it is Kapha that provides the fat and tissue we need to keep warm. All bodily fluids are regulated by Kapha, which is rather a lot, as the body contains approximately 70%, including saliva and digestive juices.

Mentally, Kapha governs our ability to remain grounded and create stability as well as security in our lives. Our ability to create structure and our capacity to keep stable and calm, feel empathy and be reflective, kind and secure, is regulated by Kapha.

The three doshas in our physical and mental constitution

To understand how these three principles affect us, we can look at how they appear in our physical and mental profile, since most of us are a mix of the different features. As you go through the paragraphs below, consider which of the various characteristics belonging to Vata, Pitta and Kapha apply to you, and your own personality type will become apparent.

Vata people

People affected by Vata are those whose physical composition is narrow and thin. Either they are tall and narrow or short and thin, and when in balance they display wit and openness. Their subcutaneous layer of fat is thin. They are fast and agile in both thought and action. They quickly and creatively initiate new projects, but before long, they lose interest and start looking for the next, new project. They are not interested in long-term management, and rather see themselves as innovators initiating new thinking and innovative approaches. Those governed by Vata exhaust easily and are prone to feel the cold. Ideally, they would prefer to eat little and often and skipping a meal can make them feel weak and make their blood pressure drop. There is a physical and mental agility to them and their most striking feature is their problem-solving skills. They dislike being still, preferring physical activity, walking quickly and are light underfoot. Mentally, they have an ongoing thinking process and creative ideas come frequently and fast. They are flexible and like change.

Generally, they prefer to be around people and often feel the need for social interaction. Prominent traits in people governed by Vata include creativity as well as being service-minded and attentive and they commonly seek employment requiring these particular qualities. They swing between swift decision making and irresolution whereby the decision-making process is filled with angst as they often end up thinking too much about what is right and wrong, and what other people will think.

Problem-solving strategies of those ruled by Vata

Vata people's thinking patterns tend to be changeable. They are quick to change their mind and often see new opportunities, which has a tendency to frustrate other personality types. The constant feeling of unease and anxiety hovering within, will surface immediately under pressure and in stressful times. Their moods might be changeable; being in a good mood one day and a bad mood the next. If they get angry they will calm down as quickly as they erupt into anger. Since their keywords are speed and change, their conflicts and disagreements follow a similar pattern.

Activity patterns of those dominated by Vata

Vata people tend to be irregular in nature and they like to be spontaneous doing different things. They also like to have the freedom to express their spontaneity and creativity, but need a clear structure in which to operate, so that they know exactly what is expected of them. Boredom tends to set in easily if they have to keep doing the same thing time and again.

Those governed by Vata quickly becoming anxious and nervous when exposed to too much inconsistency, stress and agitation. Vata people tend to be more fragile than the other personality types, reacting negatively to stress and pressure much faster. Their self-confidence is usually not as strong and powerful as that often enjoyed by those governed by Pitta, resulting in Vata people needing reassurance and encouragement to feel that they are good enough and that they are on the right track. Vata people will succeed in sports requiring speed and agility. For example, ballet, figure skating, gymnastics and high jump would suit Vata personalities, while some marathon runners are thin Vata persons, with a strong Pitta, representing their endurance and relentlessness.

Pitta people

The body size of those dominated by Pitta is generally medium. They may have bright, slightly red, sensitive skin and they usually dislike too much heat and burn easily in the sun. They have a lot of energy and radiate passion and joy when they are in balance. Their digestive system is strong, which means that they prefer regular meal times, or they tend to become irritated or even angry.

Pitta people are ambitious, which they utilise for setting and achieving goals. They can be sharp, analytical and driven. Generally, they are very goal oriented and focused with an inherent ability to take charge. They are usually fast and convincing when making decisions and they easily move from words to action.

Achieving their goals reassures them, and they thrive in situations where they are able to influence and be in charge in different ways. They are generally more explosive in both joy and anger.

Problem-solving strategies of those dominated by Pitta

When a person who is dominated by Pitta is confronted, irritation and frustration usually ensue, as a person dominated by Pitta usually has no problem expressing such feelings. They easily take any irritation out on those around them and they usually want to be on the right side of an argument. They have strong opinions and before being persuaded they require firm evidence and will often get to the bottom of any issue at hand. Sometimes they do not have the patience to be flexible and easy-going.

Activity patterns of those dominated by Pitta

Those dominated by Pitta are usually goal-oriented and once they have found a meaningful goal, they will stop at nothing to achieve it. They really enjoy creating structures, schedules and taking control of their activities and generally need to see clear results of their efforts. Pitta people are more independent and usually very self-confident and their need for assurance from others is not as pronounced as for the other doshas, rather their need lies in wanting to see their own results. They do not mind being straightforward and dare to go against the grain. More often than others, they view life as a struggle. In sports, they are often individualistic and work really hard for results. Sports such as tennis, golf, soccer and even ice-hockey are dominated by Pitta people. Many world class skiers are a mixture of the seriously goal oriented Pitta, and Kapha with its strong endurance.

Kapha people

Those dominated by Kapha are people whose body, by nature, is larger. They are generally taller than average and their physique is bigger. They have a slightly paler complexion and their connective tissue is plumper and they have more subcutaneous fat. They radiate security and harmony, and often take a methodical approach to things which means that they take "one thing at a time." Their tempo is slower than for those dominated more by Vata and Pitta. Their digestive system is slower, which can result in them gaining weight more easily. They do not have strong hunger signals and sometimes eat only twice a day and still feel satisfied. They give themselves time to reflect.

Mentally, Kapha people exude stability and calm that they spread to those around them. They have a natural ability to listen and possess great empathy and understanding. They thrive on caring for others and like to have time to think and rest. They may be perceived as more introverted as they do not talk as much as those dominated by the other doshas.

Problem-solving strategies of those dominated by Kapha

Those dominated by Kapha do not succumb to stress or pressure as they prefer to avoid a lifestyle that involves excessive stress and conflicts. Intrinsically they covet peace and understanding between people. Under pressure they react by withdrawing and becoming even more quiet and introverted. They need time for reflection and consideration before making decisions, and feel uncomfortable if they are "forced" to make decisions or answer questions under duress when they are not prepared.

Activity patterns of those dominated by Kapha

Those dominated by Kapha often live a peaceful and stable life with their routines firmly in place. They generally thrive when life stays pretty much the same as usual. If they are building a house, raising children or making important decisions at work, they tend to do so methodically and calmly. "One thing at a time" is Kapha people's motto. Usually they are very secure in themselves, but since they are often quieter than the other two personality types, they can be regarded as insecure. They do not like a fast pace and therefore have a slightly more relaxed approach to their activities. Making changes and getting things off the ground can be an issue and may create a feeling of being stuck as they constantly need more time to reflect. In sports, Kapha is represented by people who choose sport based on strength and endurance, such as weightlifting and basketball, which are dominated by Kapha.

Different combinations

Vata - Pitta

Those whose constitution is made up the most of Vata and Pitta, are dominated by Vata's ease and changeability together with Pitta's energy of drive and focus without Pitta becoming too intrusive. There is a balance between on the one hand expressing your own ideas, and the need for being more accommodating, on the other. For them, it is more important to be perceived in a positive light by others, than pushing their own ideas despite them being the most successful. These people are characterised by flexibility and passion. Thanks to Vata's flexibility these people can be good at finding their own, sometimes unconventional, ways of life without creating too much friction with their close community.

Pitta - Vata

Here, the passion and desire of Pitta dominates in combination with the ease of Vata's. These people are usually very self-confident without being dominating and constantly focused on goals. Their confidence gives them the strength to accept challenges and go for their goals. Since they possess the drive of Pitta, they have the ability to inspire others to join in the quest for their goals. People who are dominated by these two energies are fast, agile and more determined in the decisions they have to make. They are more courageous in accepting the disapproval of other people when following their heart.

Pitta – Kapha

This personality type has Pitta's will and drive along with the energy, strength, stamina and calmness of Kapha. They often have the capacity for being the perfect combination of endurance and the ability of being purposeful with a clear picture of their goals. These people are characterised by having the ability to fall and pick themselves up and try time and again.

Kapha - Pitta

Kapha-Pitta is dominated by the substance, moderation and balance of Kapha along with Pitta's fire. Those dominated by this combination have a "low intensity" approach to life and do not rush to finish things, neither are they in a hurry or motivated by time constraints. Their strength is in being mellow and having the ability to plod along quietly "beneath the surface", without needing to express their goals to get what they want. By persisting, they get where they are going in a more grounded way, as they have advanced methodically.

Kapha - Vata

This is a slightly more complex and contradictory combination because Kapha and Vata are each other's opposites. These people often find it difficult to know who they are when completing a test. On one side, they have Kapha's stillness, humility and diligence and on the other, Vata's spontaneity, openness and flexibility. They can easily adapt to new circumstances and are very accepting. Their high level of acceptance in combination with great endurance may make it difficult getting out of some circumstances in which they are not happy.

Vata - Kapha

This is also a complex constitution where Vata's ease, speed and creativity combines with its capacity for endurance, which results in staying calmer and more methodical than pure Vata people. They are more dominated by changeability, but have the ability to keep "both feet on the ground." In balance, they generally have the unique ability to utilise their creativity without creating too much chaos and inconsistency, as their Kapha-energy helps them maintain internal calmness.

Vata – Pitta – Kapha

Finally, equal amounts of all three doshas in one person is the least common combination and only found in a few people. Tradition has it that these people often are very balanced with no dosha is more dominant than another. On the other hand, if they do lose equilibrium, more care is required to regain balance. In balance, these people have access to all the good aspects of all three doshas with Vata's flexibility, Pitta's drive and the peace and stability of Kapha.

The doshas govern our body and mind

Let us take a look at how the doshas dominate and control various processes in the body and mind. Keep an eye on your most common symptoms to find out which dosha they appear in.

Vata, which governs movement and cavities found in:

- Colon
- Ear/Hearing
- Skeleton
- Peristalsis/bowel movement
- Motion of the heart
- Blinking of the eye
- The movement of blood through the body

- Pituitary/nerve tissue
- Ability to receive nerve impulses
- Respiration
-

Pitta, which governs fire and digestion and can be found in:

- Small intestine
- Eyes
- Skin
- Liver
- Heart (muscle)
- Blood
- Muscles
- Ability to evaluate and digest information from the five senses
- Metabolism/cell division
- Digestion
- Vital heat

Kapha, the qualities that lubricate and build the body, can be found in:

- Stomach
- Lungs
- Smell
- Taste
- Synovial fluid
- Mucous and mucous membranes

- Connective tissue/facia
- Fat
- Pancreas
- Lymph and all bodily fluids
- Anything having lubricating effect in the body
- Ability to build trust and stability

Dosha means "that which may be off balance." Each dosha has its own tendency to become imbalanced, which means that one particular dosha becomes excessive and the signs of imbalance are particular to each dosha. Usually, but not always, it is the dosha we are most dominated which that becomes imbalanced first. If you are governed by two doshas, you must be sure to balance both. The most active of all doshas is Vata, as it is always involved in disease and illness. Short-term issues and all symptoms that come and go, such as headaches, anxiety and back and neck pain, is mostly due to Vata.

What causes Vata to become imbalanced

Because Vata is the most fragile dosha, Vata people who are not very careful about being balanced tend to not always be in the best health. Typical Vata symptoms include backache, headache, anxiety, insomnia, menstrual pain and mood swings. Exhaustion is the result of prolonged Vata-dominance.

The main causes of Vata imbalance are:

- Long-term stress

- Exhaustion, physically or mentally
- Erratic lifestyle, especially in relation to food and sleep
- Uncertainty in life about work, finances, relationships that lead to constant worry and anxiety
- Fear of not being good enough
- Constant sensory input, for instance, excessive exposure to computer work/TV/loud music
- Excessive travel
- Periods of poor nutrition (fasting)
- Too chilly in the form of cold weather, food and drink

Symptoms when Vata is imbalanced:

- Dry skin and dry hair
- Constipation
- Wandering pains in joints and muscles
- Creaking joints
- Gassy and bloated stomach
- Pain in shoulders, neck and back
- Cold, bad blood circulation
- Sleep disturbances, very easily awakened
- Fatigue
- Restlessness
- Tinnitus
- Poor nutrition
- Osteoporosis
- Low blood pressure
- Dizziness

- Worry and anxiety
- Submission and victim mentality
- Difficulty keeping to a routine in everyday life
- Irregular and painful periods
- Less bleeding when having periods
- Anguish
- Feelings of guilt and shame
- Collapse

What causes Pitta to become imbalanced

The health of Pitta people is generally good because health and well-being is based on good digestion in ayurvedic tradition, which makes for healthy tissue, a strong immune system and natural satisfaction. Since many governed by Pitta have a strong digestive system, they are often in good health. Typical Pitta symptoms affecting young people are acne and eruptions. Other clear Pitta symptoms are gastritis, heartburn, diarrhoea and skin problems. Chronic infections and ultimately cardiovascular problems are more serious Pitta imbalances. Pitta people often keep up an intense pace and can drive themselves well beyond what is good for them and have the potential to burn themselves out. When a Pitta person becomes overly critical, cynical, dominant or very angry, these are clear signs of suppressed anger and grief which must be taken seriously.

The main causes of Pitta imbalance are:

- Stress with suppressed anger and frustration

- Prolonged time pressure
- Too strong, hot and spicy food
- Heavy alcohol consumption (like putting fuel on the fire)
- Intensive exercising without rest for a long period of time
- Constant high demands
- Constant focus on goals
- Constant need to perform and to be "best"
- Too much heat and sun

Symptoms when Pitta is off balance:

- Diahorrea
- Acne and eruptions
- Rashes
- Hot and warm
- Increased hunger and thirst
- Heartburn
- Edgy/irritable
- Gastritis/ulcers
- Infections
- Inflammation
- Vision problems
- Increased haemorrhaging
- Fever
- Headache/migraine
- Hair loss/early greying
- Cardiovascular disease
- High blood pressure due to stress and frustration

- Dominant, aggressive and critical behaviour
- Anger
- Cynicism
- Difficulty relaxing
- Excessive bleeding when having periods

What causes Kapha to become off balance

The Kapha dosha is the most stable dosha, which means that it takes a long time to become imbalanced. This also means that Kapha people can let themselves go for quite a while without experiencing any imbalances or developing symptoms. When this dosha is off balance, it is an uphill struggle to regain balance. Typical symptoms of Kapha include chronic colds, increased mucous production with blocked sinuses, obesity, swollen joints, depression and difficulty getting things done. Kapha people tend to avoid visiting the doctor at first, because they endure for a long time before seeking help.

The main causes of Kapha imbalance are:

- Foods that contain large amounts of sugar, fat or sauces
- Eating when not hungry
- Avoiding changing things that do not serve them well
- Sleeping too late in the morning during the Kapha hours (6-10 in the morning)
- Shifting the circadian rhythm, that is, going to bed late at night and sleeping in late the next day
- Lack of exercise
- Idleness, all too often choosing the easiest option

- Excessive need to provide for others
- Laziness

Symptoms of Kapha being off balance:

- Overweight/obesity
- Slow digestion
- Rarely hungry
- Inertia and inability to change
- Sinus problems and increased mucus
- Respiratory allergies/spring colds
- Asthma/bronchial problems
- Introvert and quiet
- Depression, heavy and prolonged
- Difficulty expressing feelings
- Diabetes
- Chronic fatigue due to sleeping late in the day and being up late at night
- Lack of vital heat
- High cholesterol
- High blood pressure due to bad digestion/clogged blood vessels
- Difficulty accepting change
- Difficulty getting to the point
- Prolonged bleeding during menstruation

Strengthening the doshas

Since ayurvedic tradition considers the Vata dosha the most fragile, it is also those governed by Vata who find themselves unbalanced most easily. They are often thought to have twice the amount of symptoms than those dominated by Pitta. Kahpa, on the other hand, is the most resilient and has the strongest dosha. Because of Kapha´s strong dosha they are sick less often and usually express fewer symptoms. Should Kapha lose balance, it takes time to regain balance because this dosha is very slow by nature. Vata symptoms, on the other hand, appear and disappear quickly or come and go at an irregular pace. When they appear, Pitta symptoms are more intense and tend to be more serious as bleeding can occur.

Aided by the test, you are beginning to learn which dosha you have the most, the second most and the least of, or if you have two doshas that dominate. If your personality comprises a lot of Vata, it is this dosha that run the risk of becoming imbalanced first and you would begin to experience symptoms such as wandering pains, cracked skin, constipation, and mental confusion and fatigue. If you are governed by Pitta, it will become imbalanced first and you would begin to experience Pitta-type symptoms such as skin problems, haemorrhage, diahorrea, gastritis, irritation and suppressed frustration. Should you be governed by Kapha, it would become imbalanced first and symptoms would include heaviness, obesity, mucous production, sinus congestion, lethargy and melancholy. Of course, anybody can have all the different symptoms, but if you take a look at them all, you should be able see your own symptom and illness pattern emerge.

Everyone is predisposed to certain diseases, which is in our genes and the result of the lifestyles of our ancestors. With the help of Ayurveda, we can gain a better understanding of which type of health issues we are predisposed to. The beauty of it is that our personality traits also predispose us to certain strengths that help keep us strong and healthy. I suggest that you focus on them! Shortly, we will take a look at how we can balance ourselves to increase our well-being.

Begin by observing how you feel, what symptoms you may have and link them with the dosha to which they belong. Then look at what dosha you are governed by and check if you can start joining the dots when you notice a repeating pattern. Nothing is left to chance. Feeling unwell is a message that everything is not right. The sooner we learn to listen to and identify our imbalances, the faster we are able to regain balance. Listen, pause and start taking care of yourself!

Creating balance

What should we do if we want to take care of ourselves and create balance and well-being?

First of all, we must acknowledge that it is normal to feel good; that is, essentially, our normal state. It is actually normal to feel really good and experience pleasure and a zest for life. Feeling unwell, being sick, going through a crisis or a rough patch in life is also quite normal, but it is not where we should stay. Our body and mind have excellent resources for balance and well-being, as long as we give ourselves the opportunity. Listen to what your body and mind are trying to tell you. Feeling good should not be a struggle, just as a child should not struggle to grow, or a flower to bloom. It does help if you have the ability to adopt an attitude which would help you create well-being in your life fairly effortlessly. Change always starts in your thoughts and your internal image of yourself and your well-being.

The most important question is, what you should do more or less of, in order to get there.

Ayurvedic tradition stipulates that you should always balance the dosha you have got too much of. If you are experiencing Pitta-type symptoms, it means you have too much Pitta in your constitution. In that case you need to balance Pitta. The same goes for too much Vata or Kapha.

Everything around us affects us, but the question is in what way. Everything can be categorised into Vata, Pitta and Kapha. The weather can be governed by Vata, Pitta or Kapha, time may be governed by Vata, Pitta or Kapha, the food you eat can be governed by Vata, Pitta or Kapha, and so on. The trick is to understand what affects you, which quality it is based on according to the three doshas, so that you can begin to re-balance. Stress, for example, is Vata with too much movement. Excessive stress will give you Vata symptoms sooner or later, no matter what your dominating dosha is, and you would need to balance Vata.

I often speak about life skills, which is the most efficient form of self-management, providing the foundation for continuous wellness. We will look at the biggest and most profound things affecting us on a daily basis, which fortunately you can begin to master immediately.

Life skills means becoming aware of:

- Breathing: if you do not breathe for a few minutes, you die.
- Liquid: if you do not drink for a few days, you die.
- Food: if you do not eat within a few weeks, you die.

1. Breath is the life force Prana, as it is known in the ayurvedic tradition. It is also known as Qi or Ki in Chinese and Japanese traditions, and is what provides you with your life energy. Your breath can either fill you with power and energy, or push you down and create anxiety. Think about when you exercise, and your breath is just flowing, satisfying your need for oxygen. Or while quietly meditating, relinquishing control of your breathing completely, allowing everything to synchronise perfectly. Inhaling vigorously replenishes nutrition within the cells and removes toxins, including helping the body rid itself of carbon dioxide. Under stress, we tend to breathe lightly and shallowly which does not satisfy our need for oxygen. Panic attacks are actually battles in which we fear deep down for our own life. Today, having panic attacks is a common health issue which is on the increase as the pace of our lives increases. Take a moment to consider how you breathe.

Give yourself the opportunity to fill yourself with lots of Prana by dropping everything for a moment. Relax your face, mouth and tongue. Make sure you have relaxed your jaw enough to not clench your teeth and now... BREATHE. Take some nice, relaxing breaths and replenish with exactly what you need – life energy! Return to this super simple exercise as often as you need.

2. As I mentioned before, the body consists of more than 70% water. It is a dominant part of us. Water that stands still stagnates, while water that flows clear creates life. The same applies to our bodily fluids. They want to circulate. Exercise is one of the easiest ways to increase flow and circulation. Regular exercise helps you balance both your body and your mind, as well as removing toxins and carbon dioxide while replenishing oxygen. Ayurveda has a further trick for maintaining regular circulation to keep tissues and blood vessels "clean" through drinking boiled warm water regularly. It is completely safe, has no side effects and is usually free. Boil some water and drink about 6-8 cups by the mouthful, as hot as you are comfortable with, each day. Please note that you should not mix boiled water with "raw" tap water. Most likely you would like the water at a different temperature depending on the season and it is important to do what feels best at any given time. On a hot day, you probably want your water at room temperature and if it is cold during the winter, you might

want it hot, especially if you are dominated by Vata. Pitta people should be careful to not drink it too hot and Kapha people should drink a maximum of 6 cups of boiled water per day, since they already have a lot of fluid in their bodies. Never put boiled water in the fridge to cool it down though, since any refrigerated drinks will slow down the digestive process.

3. The food you eat provides the building blocks and renews your tissue. Think about how that sandwich you just held in your hand will break down in your stomach and intestines without you having to think or do anything, and be transformed into a new part of you. Is it not absolutely fantastic! We will look more at food later on. In short, the food you are eating is a way of giving yourself love. What types of food would you like to become new tissue in your body? Pure, organic, additive-free food, as unprocessed as possible, are best for your digestive system, as it is the kind of food we have eaten for hundreds and thousands of years. The more artificial food we ingest, the greater the risk for all sorts of symptoms and diseases: obesity, diabetes, hypertension and high lipid levels being just a few of the symptoms associated with what we eat.

These three areas are easy to apply to create balance in our daily life: we need to breathe, drink and eat every day, so you will have plenty of opportunity to practice. Ayurveda provides many exercises and daily habits, but nothing that you must follow obediently. In Ayurveda nothing is black or white, the whole philosophy is very pragmatic and is based more on testing and feeling. What matters is what you experience. If you feel better after trying out some of the advice in this book, you are on the right track. If you feel worse, just stop whatever it is you are trying. Remember when trying out a new habit that it takes 21 days to replace the old habit with a new one. The body needs 21 days to get used to a new habit and whichever new routine you would like to try, continue for at least 21 days before evaluating whether it gave you what you were hoping for. If it did not appear to make any difference for you, you then need to decide whether to continue or not. Remember that if you never try anything, you will never find out if it would work.

If you have decided to give yourself the opportunity to feel better, make a decision now. Ask yourself how good you would like to feel. Will you continue to keep your nose above the parapet, just surviving, or would you like to live a life filled with vitality and love, that you have the time and ability to extend to others?

The choice is yours. What is your favourite obstacle for not allowing yourself to feel 100%? Let us start by looking at the simple areas you need help with in your everyday life for balancing Vata, Pitta and Kapha.

Regularity – balances Vata

The main theme for bringing order and balance to Vata is *regularity*. Those governed by Vata enjoy variety and change, and can therefore easily create a life with too much change, which creates stress, anxiety and confusion. Since this dosha is the most fragile, a Vata person cannot let themselves go for very long before they develop symptoms, and above all, anxiety will promptly appear on the scene. It may seem a bit boring to tell a Vata person to create more regularity in their life, but it is precisely their ability to create these conditions that will allow them to be more changeable and flexible in general. To safeguard, feeling good means creating greater flexibility and endurance which is important for Vata individuals. It is particularly important for a Vata person to follow their natural rhythm and eat, sleep and workout at regular times.

Simple tips and advice:

- Make sure you get enough sleep, go to bed by 10 pm at the latest.
- Meditate regularly, once a day.
- Add heat in the form of boiled hot water and food, especially during winter.
- Take saunas or hot baths regularly.
- If you have been through a very stressful period, compensate with rest and tranquillity, avoid too many impressions like listening on high music, watching movies, while you recover.
- Moisture the body each morning with sesame oil, preferably after a warm shower is particularly good for Vata. See Appendix for oil massage.

- Since Vata people tend to worry and feel anxious, it is a challenge for them to accept that life is unpredictable. By taking control of what you can control, such as your daily routines, you will increase your ability to feel secure and confident.

Moderation - balances Pitta

The main theme for bringing order and balance to Pitta is *moderation*. It probably would not be much fun for a person governed by the Pitta personality, who is passionate, excessive and temperamental, to be told that they must become more moderate. Yet this is their golden opportunity to achieve lifelong health. For Pitta, it is about remaining balanced while being "excessive", so to speak. Pitta people are easy to spot. When they are hungry, they are ravenous, when they are in love, they are hot and passionate, when they are motivated in their job, they can work all hours, and so on, which is both their strength, but also their weakness. To allow passion to flow when the desire hits you, you must be careful and do things in moderation in your day to day life. Pitta people are the ones at risk of burning out (or wearing others out) because they can go well beyond their own limits. It is even more important for those having a combination of Vata and Pitta to look after themselves, as fragility becomes more pronounced the more Vata is present. The opportunity for Pitta people to balance themselves, involves learning to enjoy doing nothing. It may sound ridiculous, I know, but Pitta people tend to do more than just be. They like to cram things in and constantly fill their calendars to the brim to do even more. They need to set time aside to do nothing apart from just enjoy being. Meditation is a great way to create Pitta balance, although it can be a challenge, as there is always a risk that people dominated by Pitta will view meditation as another thing to accomplish. Soon enough, they will define meditation as good or bad, and that is when it is time to watch out. Relax and let go of the need to assess and analyse everything, which is a favourite Pitta pastime. The main theme for those governed by Pitta is to find a balance between activity and rest.

Simple tips and advice:

- Make time for unwinding after periods of high tension.
- Any form of cooling off, cool boiled water, cold bedroom, cold showers.
- Eat cool food that is not too hot and spicy, especially if you have Pitta symptoms. Cold salad works well, especially in the summer. Be sure to eat and drink in moderation.
- If you are constantly hungry, try to balance by drinking cooled, boiled water by the mouthful throughout the day.
- Be careful with artificial heat, such as alcohol, coffee and other stimulants.
- If you have skin problems, it is particularly important to stick with clean food, free from toxins and pesticides, as much as possible.
- Make sure to exercise in moderation, beware of exhaustion.

- Since Pitta people tend to take life very seriously, humour is one of the best ways to bring Pitta down to a level that creates well-being. Challenge yourself to choose that which fills you with joy.
- Suppressed anger and frustration are like ticking bombs, so be sure to sort out what you need to sort out, and practice acceptance and forgiveness.

Stimulation - balancing Kapha

The main theme Kapha is to balance between stimulation and activity. The Kapha energy properties include calmness, consistency and slowness. Therefore, those governed by Kapha tend to be slow, take time before making decisions and can have difficulty getting things off the ground. For Kapha people to achieve long-term wellbeing, they must always be sure to create activity and stimulation in their lives. The most important thing is to partake in high-intensity physical activity several times a week and to reach a level where they start perspiring. Kapha people tend to establish comfortable, but not always healthy, habits that they like to cling to. To create balance, be sure to change those old patterns and habits that are not always sustainable. As Kapha needs time to take in impressions, digest, reflect and find new opportunities, it is important for the Kapha person to occasionally do things differently. To ensure they do not get stuck in stagnation and melancholy, they need to challenge their lifestyle choices. They may need to take charge of potential weight issues, as those dominated by Kapha often are predisposed to putting on weight easily due to the slowness of their digestive system. An important factor for creating balance in Kapha people is to ensure that their digestive fire is in balance, which simply means ensuring that they get hungry before meals.

Simple tips and advice:

- Be sure to create variety in life and work, and dare to challenge old habits.
- Eat the right amount and no more than three times a day. Make sure you are hungry before meals.
- Cut back on sweet and fatty foods (if you have a tendency towards being overweight) because these flavours increase Kapha. We will look into this more in the food chapter.
- Eat more hot and spicy food. Ginger is very good as it speeds up digestion.
- Drink about six cups of boiled, warm water throughout the day.
- Heat, because the Kapha dosha is cold. Dry heat is the best choice so choose dry sauna over steam bath or a hot shower rather than hot baths, and so on.
- Exercise, exercise, exercise, regularly. Preferably every day, but at least four times a week. Getting sweaty will clear out excess Kapha.
- Start listening to your body: if you are ill, make sure you recover; if you start getting stuck and feel heavy, make sure you exercise or activate yourself.

- The feeling of being stuck is devastating; be sure to get support and help getting out of situations you are not comfortable in, be it a marriage, job, relationship, or any other situation you have endured for too long.

Conclusion

As you can probably begin to see, there is a pattern to this jumble of Vata, Pitta and Kapha. Vata people need to create more structure, tranquillity and stability, which is the exact opposite of what Kapha people need. Kapha people need activity, exercise and change, especially when it comes to lifestyle. Pitta people need to pay attention to their inclination to go from use to abuse, whatever it may be, as passion and drive always form part of their personality. Therefore, they must ensure that they are in control of their behaviour so they can stop in time. Clearly, all these qualities can be found in everyone. Hopefully, by now you can see that you have a pattern that you are governed by without having to think about it.

This book is all about becoming more focused and aware of patterns and behaviours in order to understand what we can do more of and what we should cut back, in order to create more vitality and wellbeing. We can only begin to control that which we are aware of. Many of my students say that they felt a sense of relief realising and understanding their personality types, as they have gained a greater understanding of what it is that affects them. Understanding your personality means realising that it has both strong and weak traits. It also means that you will have a greater understanding of the people you meet. Having knowledge of Vata, Pitta and Kapha provides clarity about what we can actually do, to affect our daily lives. The smarter the choices you make in your life, the more you can live for, rather than against, your life. The first step toward change is gaining understanding and insight. Then you must take on board that you cannot change everything. Accept what you cannot change and start changing that which you actually can change. Embrace the power of who you are and understand that you have every opportunity to create a good life for yourself. Remember that our internal thoughts on repeat will manifest in the external world. Look for role models, those you see who seem to enjoy life, feel good and have found a way of life that moves them forward. Be sure to be influenced by them, and you will be on your merry way.

Coaching tips

- *Use the test to identify your constitution.*
- *Identify your most common symptoms, and see which dosha is most off balance.*
- *Set a goal for how good you want to feel, be as descriptive as possible.*
- *Try a maximum of three tips for balancing the dosha that you are expressing the most symptoms of.*
- *Remember that it takes 21 days to change a habit, so let 21 days pass before evaluating the results*

3

Rhythm of life

"If you think too long about the next step, you will end up standing on one leg in life."

Chinese proverb

All life follows a rhythm, the rhythm of day and night and of seasons that come and go. All humans are part of this natural rhythm. Modern man, Homo Sapiens, has inhabited Earth for approximately 200,000 years and mankind has existed for the past 2 million years. Throughout, we have been characterised by the continual rhythm encompassing everything. Once a day, Earth revolves around its own axis and around the Sun in a year, a rhythm that has been programmed into our cells since the beginning of time. This means that every living thing has been programmed with its own rhythm since the outset. Birds wake up at dawn and start chirping, they do not have lie-ins and begin to chirp at 11.00 in the morning! The flowers know when to bloom and animals are aware of when they should start storing food for winter. When we follow our internal, natural rhythm, well-being comes to us effortlessly. It happens spontaneously as soon as we give it space.

Two significant modern time events have severely impacted our natural rhythm. One was when we invented electricity. Suddenly, at a flick of a switch, we could switch on a lamp and stay up at night despite our bodies being used to sleeping. The other major event was introducing the international standard time system. Different time zones were established in different parts of the world and we introduced the use of clocks instead of following our natural rhythm. Modern society has the option of eating at any time of day and to be awake for as long as we like at night, sleep during the day and disrupt virtually all our natural rhythms. Our natural daily rhythm is called the circadian rhythm and is the rhythm our bodies and cells follow. Research has shown that almost all human physiological and biochemical processes follow a regular circadian rhythm. Many of these phenomena, such as pulse, mental and physical activity, as well as digestive processes and adrenaline levels, peak during the day and slow down during the dark hours. Other processes, such as those controlling melatonin levels, growth hormones, cholesterol and sex hormones peak at night. The immune system is most active at night and our response mechanism and speed are best during the afternoon.

Ayurveda has a long tradition of understanding and utilising the healing powers of the circadian rhythms. To create balance in your life, it is important to take into account the circadian, as well as the seasonal rhythms. The rhythms we are most aware of include sleeping, eating, bowel movements, menstruation cycles, working patterns, rest and activity rhythms, although everything we do and all our physical and mental processes are parts of a larger rhythmic context. The three energies Vata, Pitta and Kapha can be found in everything and we can study the times each day when each of the energies is most dominant.

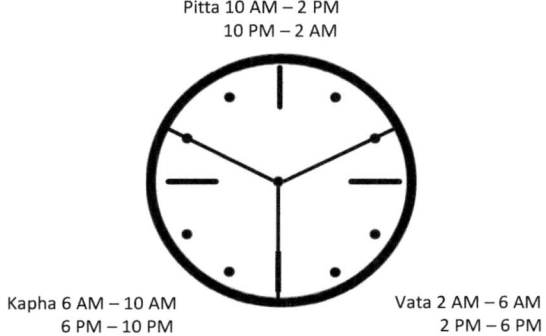

Pitta 10 AM – 2 PM
10 PM – 2 AM

Kapha 6 AM – 10 AM
6 PM – 10 PM

Vata 2 AM – 6 AM
2 PM – 6 PM

Vata time, 2 am - 6 am and 2 pm - 6 pm

The influence of Vata is greatest in the afternoon between 2 and 6 and during the night between 2 and 6. During Vata time we are governed by movement and change. It is during these hours at night when we are in what is referred to as REM sleep, when our sleep is at its most shallow and dreams are abundant. During the early morning hours our sleep progressively becomes more and more shallow until, finally, we wake up. It is also during Vata time of day that the body moves toxins to the organs of elimination to be prepared to leave your body in the morning when you wake up. Vata energy is active also in the afternoon between 2 and 6 which keeps us quick and witty and, according to research into the biological clock, this is the time of day our response time is the fastest.

Pitta time, 10 am – 2 pm and 10 pm – 2 am

Pitta time represents digestion, both physically and psychologically. Some times around noon, when the sun is at its highest, is when our digestion is the most active. Most people are the hungriest around noon which is when our ability to digest the food we ingest is naturally at its most effective. Educators have found that our capacity for learning math, languages and making the most use of our intellect, is also during this time. Pitta represents our ability to digest external impressions, specially from our sight, as well as our ability to analyse and focus.

Between 10 and 2 at night, Pitta can be found transforming our organs to enable them to remove waste and generate new tissue. An internal anabolic process within is activated during Pitta time of night to generate new tissue and help us recover from the break down process that is in force when we are awake and active during daytime. The later, past 10 pm that we get to sleep, the less advantage we can take of this regeneration process. A lot of us get a second wind if we stay up later than 10.30 to 11pm and can suddenly stay up, work and be active late into the night. It is the active part of Pitta that reveals itself and gives us renewed energy. However, avoiding taking advantage of this time for sleep and recovery has the potential to cause long-term damage. It is like burning a candle at both ends. Staying up late every once in a while, is not a problem, but letting it becomes a way of life is.

Kapha, 6 am - 10 am and 6 pm - 10 pm

These time slots represent calmness and restraint, in body as well as mind. When we wake up in the morning, most of us feel a bit sluggish before we get going, and anyone dominated by Kapha often feel worse than others. The next phase of Kapha starts to emerge around 6 in the evening and is the time we progressively begin feeling more and more heavy and calm, making most of us tired enough to want to go to bed at about 10-11 pm. The evening is the time for getting some peace and quiet and to reflect and socialise before going off to bed.

Consider the daily rhythms

To effortlessly create wellbeing, it is important to pay attention to, and increasingly live in tune with, the different circadian rhythms as these rhythms provide the blueprint for our cells. Take a moment to think about how you follow the rhythms.

- What time do you usually wake up? How do you feel?
- Are you hungry in the morning? If you are not hungry, do you still eat?
- Are you hungry for lunch?
- Do you snack during the day? How does that make you feel?
- Are you highly stressed? What time do you feel most stressed?
- How late do you eat in the evening?

- What do you do at night before you go to bed?
- When do you go to bed?
- What are your sleeping patterns? Do you sleep all night long? If you wake up, what time do you usually wake up?

If we have ignored the natural rhythms for too long, eventually it will feel natural to be in an unnatural circadian rhythm. Have we not had a natural food rhythm, maybe we do not feel hungry when the body should be fed. If our sleep rhythm has been disturbed over a long period of time, it is difficult to get natural and revitalising sleep. A tip to get you started is to just observe your own rhythms and how you feel at different times during the day. When do you feel better and perhaps when do you feel worse? When do you feel full of vitality and when do you feel tired and sluggish?

Since we have lived in tune with the rhythms of the Earth since time immemorial, our rhythm follows the seasons as Earth circles around the Sun. Since everything influences us, we will all be affected more or less by season and different weather conditions, depending on our constitution.

Seasons

Summer – late summer

This season is dominated by Pitta energy, and the warmer and hotter it is, the more we are affected by Pitta. The heat can make Pitta people uncomfortable and increases the risk of disturbing Pitta and Pitta type symptoms, such as infections, fevers and inflammation.

As it becomes warmer, it is easier for us to digest cold food and drinks, and most of us adjust our eating habits naturally as we then prefer cooling foods and drinks. You will be affected more by Pitta if you live in the tropics, where eating a lot of fruit and raw vegetables is in harmony with local conditions.

Fall – winter

This season is dominated by the cold and windy energy of Vata. If it is also raining and wet outside, some Kapha energy can lead us to catching colds. During winter, increased discomfort including wandering pains, dry skin and constipation can be experienced by those governed by Vata.

Spring

Spring is dominated by Kapha; once the snow has melted nature becomes wet. This is the time when nature wakes up and everything begins to sprout and grow again. Kapha stands for expansion and some people experience the excess of Kapha in the form of spring allergies, with increased mucous production, a runny nose and eyes. Spring time depression is something that has been talked about for a long period of time and it is mostly those whose constitution is governed by Kapha who are at risk of suffering.

Balancing the effects of the seasons

Take note of your wellbeing depending on the season and weather conditions. I do not completely agree with the Swedish saying that "There are no bad weather conditions, just bad clothes", since we are affected, both consciously and unconsciously, by weather, light and changes in temperature. Light, for instance, affects our hormone production. It is well known that the warm foehn winds sweeping over the Alps have always affected the mood swings of those who live there. Those dominated by Vata are generally also those affected the most by weather conditions, as Vata is the most sensitive dosha.

We cannot control the seasons. We can, however, balance and compensate for any seasonal disturbances depending on which dosha we are governed by and the season we are in. The trick is to take extra care to nurture the dosha you are most affected by, in any particular season. If you are governed by Vata, it is extra important to keep to your daily routines during the winter, as this season is represented by Vata. Eating warm food, dressing warmly, taking hot baths, regularly drinking warm boiled water as well as eating, drinking and exercising, in tune with the natural rhythms of the day. Should you be governed by Pitta, you will need to compensate for the heat you are exposed to during summer time. The hotter it is, the more active Pitta will be. Eat and drink cool foods and liquids and exercise during the cooler hours of the day. If you are dominated by Kapha, spring energy will affect you the most, and it is essential that you pay attention to any hunger signals and only eat when you are hungry. Using a neti pot, a nose rinsing pot, to rinse your nose is a simple way of reducing mucus formation and any hay fever symptoms. Getting up before Vata-time has passed, by 6 – 6.30 in the morning to do some exercise, is another effective way of reducing the influence of Kapha. This will stimulate and move things around, to avoid stagnation of Kapha energy.

The rhythm of life through our lifetime

We acquired our constitution, together with our unique personal rhythm, at the point of conception. In the beginning, we were just a single cell containing all our information, genes and preconditions, and many different things have influenced our personal constitution. To begin, the quality of the ovum and sperm affects the quality of the embryo. And then we lived inside someone else for about nine months, a woman with her own life rhythm, balance or imbalance, and her own preconditions for creating well-being and nutrients for the fetus. Eventually we arrive into a world which will affect us in different ways. From the moment of conception until the day we stop growing in our late teens, all constitutions are dominated by Kapha, since Kapha governs everything that grows and expands. Our growth and development are dependent on the preprogramed life process that is present in all living things. Those whose constitutions are dominated by Kapha may, while growing up, have been large and slightly overweight. When they eventually enter the Pitta period in adolescence, many discover that their weight levels out.

The Pitta period emerges gradually during teenagerhood and continues up to the time that old age sets in, after age 50 to 55. Pitta energy represent implementation and realisation. During this period of time we expand our knowledge and understanding, we build family structures and social networks. We get an education, work and push ourselves closer to our goals in life. At around 45-55, when Pitta is the most active, we run the risk of experiencing the most disturbances in the Pitta energy, especially if our constitution is governed by Pitta. Any Pitta imbalance mostly makes itself known through major health issues, such as cardiovascular disease, stroke, hypertension, gastritis and ulcers, unfortunately all too common these days. On the other hand, had we been gentle on ourselves, we might have mastered the art of balancing work and rest, keeping us vital, well and full of life.

It is when our body and mind begin to grow old, that we enter the Vata period. The Vata period represents anything broken down and eliminated by the body, which is precisely what happens as we age. Increasingly, cells are broken down, our hair falls out, we often lose weight and we may even lose our memory. If we have looked after ourselves well, we can reap what we have sown during our life. Old age sometime represents love and caring for loved ones, but it can also be a time for contemplation, reflection and becoming more spiritual. We may have been accumulating too much Vata energy, if our constitution is governed by Vata, and we might run the risk of succumbing to common age related Vata imbalances, such as pain, memory loss, confusion and dementia.

To live in tune with a natural rhythm

The natural state of mankind is being completely healthy and by that, I mean not just living a life free of disease, but keeping your body, mind and spirit healthy and balanced. In fact, humans are not only created to be healthy, but also to live an abundant life flowing with love, sex, care and with enough food to keep well.

Göran Burenhult, Professor in Archaeology at Gotland University, has given a face to the topic of evolutionary medicine. He has studied archaeological sites and describes how people lived in the past. Through studying the living conditions of ancient cultures still living the way our ancestors did thousands of years ago, Prof. Burenhult and others with him have been able to demonstrate what a natural lifestyle, suitable for us humans, would entail. After years of study by him and his colleagues, including the population of the Trobriand Islands in the South Pacific, there is no doubt that many of these cultures, despite reaching the age of 90, are free of disease, myopia and age-related dementia. They still abide by a generally long forgotten but essential piece of human wisdom, wisdom which would serve us well to learn and bring into our own lives. The only thing required is that you dare try it out for a while, to find out if it will empower you.

No comprehensive research results or analyses are needed for you to discover what makes you feel good or bad. To live in tune with your natural rhythms involves navigating your everyday activities as far as you can, to suit your own natural rhythm. Doing this helps create the space to live with, and not against, the natural processes that exist within us. Most likely you will notice any changes as soon as you start to relax and stop resisting the natural rhythm of life.

Advice for following the rhythm of time

Ayurvedic tradition describes procedures you can try out, for living in harmony with the natural rhythms of life. You decide if any of them suits you.

1. Get up before Vata time is completely over (about 5.30-6.30 am) to bring the ease and energy of Vata with you into the morning. You have likely noticed Vata's awareness on occasions when you have woken up feeling really refreshed by 4 o'clock in the morning, only to fall back asleep again until 8 or 9 am and feeling quite drowsy on waking. By then, your sleep has crept into Kapha time and been exposed to the sluggishness and laziness of Kapha, which tends to stay with you well into your day.

2. Acquire simple and energising morning routines, setting the scene for your body and soul to wake up together.

   - The first thing to do in the morning is to drink boiled water (Pitta should drink cooled water).
   - Take a shower to invigorate your energy. If your constitution is in excess of Pitta, finish off with a cold shower.
   - Those with Vata and Pitta constitutions would do well to rub sesame oil onto their body. If you are able to find Vata or Pitta oil then use that. For anyone governed by Kapha, people whose skin is a bit more oily, avoid the oil and dry-brush your body instead in order to invigorate the energies.
   - Do some simple exercises for a few minutes, such as a simple yoga session, some qigong movements, or any other exercise you are familiar with, for a few

minutes. Doing this will make you feel more harmonious.

- If you want to reinforce any positive intentions and goals you have set yourself for the day, you can end your morning session by looking at a vision board you have created. See more about the vision board in Chapter 8. Your entire morning session including shower, massage, some exercises and visualisation to finish off, will take between 30-60 minutes, depending on which level you would like your energy for the day to reach. This is where you create a buffer for any stress you may encounter during the day and increase your vitality.

- Have a quiet and peaceful breakfast according to your own constitution (requires waking up in time). Suggestions on food will be given in Chapter 5.

- Have lunch according to your constitution and pay attention to any hunger signals which usually appear around 11.30-12.30 am, assuming you have not snacked during the morning.

- Balance and manage your time during the afternoon to give yourself the opportunity to take care of any stress or pressures that usually appear during Vata time in the afternoon, peaking between 5 and 6 pm.

- Between 6 and 8 pm, have a lighter meal as supper; your sleep will be more energising if you can avoid over-eating.

-   By 10-11 pm, most of us are tired and we start receiving clear signals that it is time for bed. Listen to them and get to bed on time, as going to sleep then is your best chance of creating power and energy for the next day.

Creating long-term imbalances

If you think it is too complicated to change this or that in your life, take a look at how easy it is to create imbalance.

To increase Vata symptoms, do the things on the list below:

-   Work out hard.
-   Ingest cold food and drinks, often ice-cold.
-   Be cold often.
-   Expose yourself to constant pressures and stress.
-   Expose yourself to many or continuous changes.
-   Remain in insecure life situations.
-   Put yourself in situations where you feel unloved.
-   Fly and travel as much as you can.
-   Never keep to regular routines.
-   Always feel neglected.
-   Feel sorry for yourself.
-   Always feel a victim, probably as you have been victimised the most.
-   Above all, do not sleep at night or make sure that you get irregular sleep.

-   Always remember that everyone else is right and you are probably always wrong.

To increase Pitta symptoms, do the things on the list below:

-   Expose yourself to severe stress and constant frustrations.
-   Be angry, especially in traffic jams where you cannot do anything about your situation.
-    Eat really spicy, fatty, fried and grilled food in excess.
-   Exercise to the max, no matter how many symptoms you have.
-   Always have high expectation of yourself and feel free to feel like a failure when you have not reached them.
-   Criticise and analyse most things in your surroundings and take nothing for granted.
-   Always put yourself first and make sure that you are first in line and always receive the most.
-   Sweat a lot and stay in direct sunlight for hours.
-   Make sure to always have tight deadlines and always cram too much in to your diary.
-   Use the hours between 11pm and 2 am to work to enhance your effectiveness.
-   Sleep as little as possible, to be even more efficient.
-   Rush off in the morning without having any breakfast.
-   Never encourage or declare your love to your fellow humans.
-   Always say what you think regardless and be powerful because you are always right.

To increase Kapha symptoms, do the things on the list below:

- Turn the day around and stay up all night.
- Always sleep late in the morning.
- Always eat even when you are not hungry, especially sweets and fatty things, frequently.
- Put off things until tomorrow, as often as possible.
- Provide constant care for others and feel bitter if nobody thanks you for it.
- Begrudge yourself and never get what you need.
- Never speak about your needs or ask for help.
- Never go to bed, no matter how ill you are.
- Never say what you think.
- Take a really long time to reflect before making a decision and ideally never make any decisions.
- Let everything wait.
- Sleep often and a lot during the day.

Sure, it sounds crazy, but it is only when we really acknowledge our own patterns that we realise the lifestyle we have adopted is destructive. Symptoms are just signals that something is not right, and that we often abuse ourselves. Sometimes we are aware, and sometimes we do it habitually because the pattern has become ingrained. Breaking destructive habit, takes courage and a willingness to take a look at ourselves. Far too many of us put off changing our situation, sometimes for far too long. Ayurvedic philosophy suggests that the sooner you pay attention to any imbalances, the less energy re-balancing will take. If we have neglected ourselves for a long time, of course it will take longer, but it is never too late to start over.

Coaching tips:

- *Consider if there is a certain time of day when you feel the best.*
- *Observe which time of day you feel the most resistance or symptoms.*
- *Observe, without changing anything, your particular circadian rhythm and compare with any symptoms you may have.*
- *Write down three things you are willing to change to live more in tune with your circadian rhythm.*
- *Make the decision to do one of these things and do it for 21 days. Then evaluate if it made any difference to you.*

4.

Sleep

Sound sleep prolongs life! Some researchers refer to sleep as active disconnection, whereby the brain continues to be as active as during the daytime. The function of sleep is to cleanse and refresh, to let the body regenerate, so that it can remove toxins during the night. Another function of sleep is to allow us to let go of any memories we do not need and keep those that are still useful. Dreams are still somewhat a mystery to researchers in the West, but can be described as a process facilitating the synchronisation and storage of the memories of our daytime activities. Dreams can also tell us what is going on in our subconscious. In many cultures, dreams are important and viewed as a guide for the individual. So, what is normal and vitalising sleep? To go to sleep when you go to bed, sleep through the night and wake up refreshed in the morning, which is what we were created to do, although that might not happen each night. When we reach our sixties, Vata energy increases and many suffer from disturbed sleep. Disturbed sleep is probably one of the toughest things about having young children, and the most important thing is to help our children sleep well and safely. Women's sleep patterns tend to be disrupted during their menstrual period and when they reach menopause. Sleep is regulated by hormones stimulating sleep and wakefulness, and any sleep issues are simply signals that something more deep-seated is out of balance, which in turn depends on how we live our everyday lives.

Many teenagers become increasingly tired from age 12 and as they hit puberty. Research on American teenagers claims that excessive tiredness is related to hormonal changes during growth spurts in puberty. The fact that many teenagers also change their daily rhythm does not really make for good and rewarding sleep.

Start to ask yourself the following questions:

- At what time do you get up in the morning?

- What is your morning routine?

- What do you have for breakfast? Is breakfast time relaxing or stressful?

- What do you have for lunch?

- How do you eat lunch?

- When do you have your evening meal?

- What do you do later in the evening?

- How much exercise do you get?

- How do you feel about your daytime activities? Are they meaningful?

- Do you worry about all sorts of things that you cannot or do not even want to change?

- Are you stressed or frustrated about things that you cannot actually change?

- What is your thought pattern? Is it constructive, carrying you forward, or does it hold you back, keeping you in situations you cannot influence?

- Do you regret things you cannot change?

- Do you have anxiety about the future you do not know anything about?

- What do you do each day that replenishes vitality and energy?

There are thousands of questions to ask if you want to explore your sleeping habits. The foundation for good sleep is laid during the day while a day full of vitality begins the evening before. This means that if you decide to live in tune with your natural rhythm, especially concerning sleep, food, exercise, rest and daily routines, you will establish a buffer that will keep you prepared for any challenges life has a tendency to present us with. It is rarely an issue to stray from the routine once in a while, but if you allow your life to get out of step with your natural rhythm for a longer period, soon enough symptoms will surface.

Working nightshifts is a major challenge for achieving balance in your everyday life and it is vital to get back in tune with your natural rhythm as quickly as possible. Generally, only strong Pitta-Kapha people have the capacity to handle nightshifts long-term, as their robust constitution allow them to keep off balance for a longer period of time. Although, they too will have issues, unless they do not make sure they compensate to create balance. In short, this means that the circadian rhythm should be followed as closely as possible and eating should be kept to a minimum during night-time, even at work, as the body is not able to digest food as well during the night as during the day. All stimulants such as coffee, alcohol and drugs disturb sleep to a certain degree in the long run. Usually it is Vata-people whose sleep is disturbed first, and they also have the widest range of sleep issues.

Let us begin by looking at the structure of sleep. Sleep is composed of different phases, in which the state of consciousness and muscle tension vary. Particular parts of the brain carry out different active processes, in the different phases. Sleep has been categorised into REM and NREM sleep, where REM represents Rapid Eye Movement and the lightest sleep and NREM, Non-Rapid Eye Movement, represents deep sleep. NREM has also been categorised from 1-4 where 1 represents a slumbering state and 4 deep sleep. Deep sleep is the most present during Pitta-time, between 10 pm and 2 am, which is when we get the most restorative sleep. It is worth pointing out that a person who has just fallen asleep and is woken up within 30 minutes, while still in sleep phase 1, feels as though they have not slept at all. During normal sleeping conditions, the phases are not interfered with and sleep will be fully restorative. Normal sleeping conditions is sleep that is in tune with a rhythm that has matured through evolution over hundreds and thousands of years.

Besides our living habits, the rhythm of the seasons also affects sleep and many people have probably noticed that we need more sleep during the winter months and less during the summer. Adjusting to summer or winter time will also affect sleep patterns, as will crossing time zones by air, to varying degrees. It is more common to have difficulty adjusting when flying east than flying westbound, and it is generally advisable to keep to the original time zone, if your stay in a country within a different time zone is short. If staying longer than 24 hours, try to adjust to the new time zone as quickly as possible, despite the challenge of staying awake when the natural impulse to sleep makes itself known. We progressively accumulate more Vata the more we travel, especially when crossing time zones. To compensate for the increase in Vata energy, you can reinforce any routines that brings Vata back to balance. It has been said that an 18 year old today has experienced as much as someone reaching 75 a hundred years ago, which effectively means that today we are completely bombarded with impressions, issues, thoughts about relationships and questions. We are constantly within reach of all sorts of external impressions, and consequently we are exposed to the stresses of Vata, as Vata represent impressions, movement and change. Always being online and available is an excellent way of disturbing your life rhythm. That as many as 25% of the Swedish population is said to be having sleep issues, can be viewed as evidence that we are not able to look after ourselves as well as we should. Chronic sleep deprivation means not living life to the full, that we are not able to utilise our full potential and be vital. Deciding to take charge of when to be impressionable and when you would prefer to switch off, is an effective way of creating better sleep patterns.

Lately, it has been discovered that sleep deprivation increases concentration issues, which in turn is causing a rise in accidents at work. The risk of causing an accident whilst being sleep deprived behind the wheel has been compared to driving under the influence of alcohol, while prolonged sleep issues are detrimental to good health, involving an increased risk of heart and circulation problems, diabetes and lowered immunity. We are simply made for sleeping at night and being awake during the day.

Some facts about sleep

1. *Your brain functions are enhanced.* The brain develops during sleep. Sleep deprivation makes the brain function slower during waking hours, everything seems chaotic and the level of concentration is reduced. Sufficient sleep that has gone through all the different phases makes us more efficient and makes life more enjoyable.

2. *Your memory is improved.* During sleep, unnecessary bits of memory are filtered from the important, to create more space for valuable information and avoid overloading the memory.

3. *Weight is easier to control.* Sleep deprivation makes the body cry out for fast energy. Most of us will probably recognise the cravings for junk food after a big party or night of bad sleep.

4. *You will live longer.* Serious sleep deprivation increases the risk of common health issues. For instance, research shows that the increase in stress, obesity and sleep deprivation lead to diabetes and cardiovascular disease. It is simple: good sleep will increase your health!

5. *You will be more creative.* Creativity is a state of happiness and will flow automatically if you are well rested.

6. *You will be more efficient.* In a society dedicated to efficiency, achievements – quantity being more important than quality – are highly valued. Well rested you will get more done on time.

7. *You will be more intelligent.* Sleep deprivation affects brain processes dependent on tapping into your intelligence as well as any acquired knowledge having to be applied in a new situation. Tiredness slows you down.

8. *You will learn faster.* Learning skills will improve once the brain removes any redundant memory fragments during sleep.

9. *You will be more beautiful.* The old adage that sleep makes us glow has long been known. You will radiate the benefits of good and sufficient sleep.

Ayurvedic sleep rhythms

During the deep sleep of Pitta-time, between 10 pm –and 2 am, the mind and bodily organs are busy eliminating and boosting themselves in order to improve and strengthen the immune response. This period is programmed into our cells. Making changes to this rhythm through nightshifts or doing a second shift once the kids have gone to bed, will make you go against an innate bodily process. This is not a problem, as long as it does not become a habit, and only happens once in a while. According to ayurvedic tradition, Pitta sleep is the most essential, as this period is when the body is actively reinforcing itself. Making sure you get to bed on time, before 10.30-11pm, is a very dynamic way of regaining strength after periods of excessive stress and pressure. Vata-people find themselves being most easily disrupted if out of tune with their natural rhythm. They quickly come off balance and generally it is their sleep pattern that will be disrupted the most. As a result, those governed by Vata are plagued the most by sleep issues such as too little sleep, difficulties falling asleep, nightmares, waking up in the middle of the night worrying or waking up too early and not being able to get back to sleep again. On the other hand, Kapha people tend to sleep too much and easily become night owls sleeping late into the morning. Consequently, they feel heavy and slow the next morning and it is not unusual for them to take all day to get going, not becoming active until the evening and staying awake late into the night and having to sleep in the following day. They easily end up in a Catch 22 situation. These people swiftly accumulate the heaviness of Kapha and increasingly find it difficult to get things off the ground. People governed by Kapha are those who are most subject to heavy depression.

Following a natural sleep pattern is the most important adjustment all the different personality types can make, in order to live life to the full. Do not sleep too much or too little. You will not be able to eliminate exhaustion through sleep alone and it is essential to fill up on energy boosting activities during the daytime. The sooner you revert to your own circadian rhythm, the sooner your body will be able to recover and restore itself. The transition is smooth as long as you follow the laws of nature. Listen to your body and mind guiding you toward a place of recovery and be mindful of letting yourself be led astray by wilfulness and idleness, which generally result in energy being wasted.

Our society is odd, valuing staying up late at night and sleeping in on our days off. This phenomenon is fairly unique to the western world and rarely have I heard kids in other cultures I have visited, begging to stay up late at night. On the one hand, our everyday lives revolve around getting up early and getting things done, and on the other, prioritising weekend lie-ins. Perhaps we stay up too late on Friday and Saturday, forcing the body to constantly adapt. There is a reason why heart attacks are more common on a Monday morning, as we know such differences are wearing. Partying once in a blue moon is not the problem, just do not make it a habit. It is well worth taking some time to think about these things, especially if you are having recurring issues or are ill, as they are simply different ways of boosting your energy for free. The only thing required is that you take charge and decide about what time to go to bed and what time to get up. The choice is yours.

Sleep cycles for the different doshas

Vata

To preserve health and well-being it is vital for Vata people to get eight hours of sleep a night. Getting to sleep by 10 pm and getting up around 6 in the morning is essential, as this prolongs the period of reinforcement of body and mind, since this capacity is lower in Vata than in the other two constitutions. Those governed by Vata are usually aware that they need a lot of sleep and they are usually tired at night and bright in the morning. Vata people generally wake up by themselves and are refreshed and alert when balanced. In a state of equilibrium, they are also often able to programme themselves to wake up at a certain time and frequently wake up, fairly alert, before the alarm goes off. They generally remember their dreams which are usually very active and it is not uncommon for them to dream about flying.

To recover from intensive and exhausting periods of time, everyone ought to manage their sleep properly and sleep 7 to 8 hours. Remember that having an intensive and flexible lifestyle does not mean you cannot compensate by setting time aside for daily balancing routines. My coaching clients who are burnt out have ignored physical and mental warning signs, resulting in a diminished capacity to recover. Initially, they will only be asked to stay closely in tune with the circadian rhythm and among other things pay attention to sleep.

Pitta

Pitta people like to cram things in and dislike wasting their time. Their belief that they are more efficient if they utilise every waking hour puts them at risk of burning the candle at both ends. They tend to get a second wind late in the evening, becoming alert and happily staying up working until 1-2 in the morning, if they ignore the signals telling them to get to bed. They feel really efficient but fail to understand that they are paving the way for future ill-health. Pitta people ending up chronically exhausted have missed out on the restorative Pitta-sleep that keeps the immune system strong, by ignoring any signals to go to bed, staying up late at night, too often doing jobs and keeping active. This particular process will not take place at any other time as it is an evolutionary process. It is crucial for Pitta people wanting to achieve vitality and equilibrium to be able to turn off the demands of constantly being efficient and high achieving, when they have time off. Beneficial Pitta-sleep involves 7-8 hours of sleep, ideally between 11 pm and 6 am.

Pitta people usually sleep well, and when in balance, they sleep soundly and through the night. Their dreams do not appear as frequently as for Vata people, but mostly they are colourful. Dreams can be scary for Pitta people when they are under too much stress and pressure, and can be regarded as a wake-up call during stressful periods. The challenge for Pitta people is getting to bed on time as their evenings are crammed with different activities and work. Be wary of bringing work into your bedroom, and ideally keep your desk and anything work related outside the bedroom. The bedroom is for sleeping and making love, not for work!

Kapha

As mentioned earlier, Kapha people are the ones who can easily turn the day around by falling into the habit of staying up late at night and sleeping in in the morning. They often say that their biological clock is different to everyone else's and that they are evening people by nature. Since the energy of Kapha is heavy and slow, more effort is required by a Kapha person to wake up in the morning. They are happy to stay in bed but despite doing just that, they will accumulate even more Kapha energy and getting out of bed in the morning will become more and more difficult. Ignoring the natural sleep and awake signals together with a dose of idleness makes them sleep in. Basically, if you sleep in late in the morning, you will not be tired at night, staying up until getting tired, even if that does not happen until 2-3 in the morning. The later you sleep in the morning past 7-8, the more Kapha energy will accumulate. Beneficial Kapha sleep involves 6-7 hours of sleep and it is important to watch out so you do not sleep too much.

Vata sleep disruption

Vata people are the ones most prone to unsettling their equilibrium and suffering sleep disruption. An erratic lifestyle often causes irregular sleeping patterns. The most common sleep disturbance for Vata people is difficulty in falling asleep. They either wake up anxious in the middle of the night worrying or too early in the morning and cannot get back to sleep. It is usually this people who talk and walk around in their sleep as well as waking frequently to visit the toilet at night, which increases as they age.

Panic attacks, which indicate severe Vata imbalance, will usually slowly emerge after midnight at around 2 in the morning. Panic attacks also indicate that thoughts have been allowed to take over and that you have lost control over your thoughts. This is a real problem for sufferers and the only way out is to learn to control the thoughts.

Children who wet the bed are usually Vata-children and it is vital to give them plenty of loving care and have them follow regular routines both during the day and in the evening.

Balancing Vata sleep

Keep in mind that routine is the foundation for balancing Vata, irrespective of how the imbalance occurred and the symptoms it is causing. This means that while balancing Vata you must keep to a daily routine of going to bed at the same time every night and getting up at the same time each morning. To enhance the balancing process, introduce more of that which calms Vata down, which requires setting the scene for warmth, calmness, peacefulness, and safety in preparation for the night ahead. Since Vata-people are prone to worrying about everything and nothing when they begin to become imbalanced, it is particularly important to master your thoughts. As you already know, only that which we give our focus to grows! To start, set some goals for yourself. Take time to think about how you would like to sleep. Which thoughts circle in your head when you are trying to sleep? Which thoughts would you prefer? What are your biggest fears? What is the worst thing that can happen? What would happen if you let the thoughts in, then let go of them to invite thoughts creating positive energy? The method behind mastering your thoughts involves letting go of fighting against blocking any unpleasant thoughts. The more effort we make to *avoid* thinking, the more we think and the harder we have to fight. Just let go and relax. Spend your evenings enjoying calming activities, paving the way for positive thoughts and feelings. Engage all five senses to create calmness and a safe space, listen to relaxing music, light some candles, use calming fragrances and drink a cup of hot milk with some honey and saffron. Skip watching TV while balancing your sleep since TV and computer games are Vata-enhancing activities. In fact, they consist of tiny microdots constantly moving across the screen making an impression on your mind. Finish off your evening with some breathing exercises and brief meditation.

Should you experience any imbalances other than sleep, you must of course initiate the process of balancing them too. Pain, worry, digestive problems, constant stress and dissatisfaction affects sleep negatively and begs the question, what is behind your disrupted sleep? What are you prepared to do to improve the quality of your life? How far are you prepared to go to live life to the full? Resorting to sleeping pills is a short-term solution initiating artificial sleep which does not provide the restorative sleep you require, although sometimes the chaos of life might call for them. Just make sure you do what you can to bring balance back to your life as soon as you can, to avoid having to resort to medication as they all have a certain degree of side effects.

Summary of tips for stimulating Vata sleep

- Write down what type of sleep you desire and how you would like to feel on waking.
- Write down three positive thoughts for the end of the evening. For example, 'I am completely calm and relaxed', 'I am totally safe and confident, and everything is as it should be', 'I have all I need for a sound night's sleep and to wake up refreshed tomorrow'.
- Start preparing for the night at around 9.30 pm.

- Meditate for 5-20 minutes before bed, see the Appendix at the end of the book.
- Engage all five senses to balance yourself. Hot milk with honey and saffron is particularly useful for supressing Vata energy.
- Avoid alcohol and coffee during the time you balance your sleep.
- Master your thoughts by restricting energy-sapping thoughts. Practice inviting thoughts giving you positive energy instead. The fantasies of Vata people are amazing although they can present problems for them during stressful and demanding periods, when their fantasies reach the feeling of a never-ending horror story.

It might help anyone governed by Vata that sleep disruption will affect most people dominated by Vata as soon as Vata balance is disturbed. For that reason, it is essential that you master your feelings, as they tend to run wild, creating a feeling of turbulence and insecurity around you. The easiest way to master your thoughts and emotions is in fact keeping to a routine.

Pitta sleep disruption

Pitta people generally sleep well and have a fairly regular sleep pattern. Any sleep problems usually occur because they wake up hungry, thirsty or sweating excessively in the middle of the night. Pitta sleep disruption mostly involves waking up before 2-3 in the morning. Violent dreams and nightmares can also disturb sleep.

Disrupted Pitta sleep often masks aggressive and heated emotions, emotions that are very much supressed when awake. Clenched jaws and teeth grinding are signs of too many demands and that the body is not able to relax. Since our culture does not allow such feelings, anger and aggressiveness are amongst the most difficult emotions for us to express. They represent our most basic emotions which most of us have grown up establishing different destructive ways of suppressing. Suppressed anger is like a bomb waiting to explode or implode, producing strong symptoms, in the worst-case scenario, a heart attack. Constantly thinking about work, planning meetings at night and being concerned about things that need doing are common signs of Pitta imbalance, and the challenge is to make a conscious decision about how much you will let work encroach on your private life. Generally, I say to people who tell me they are 'workaholics' that I have never heard of anyone's last wish being that they had worked more. Nevertheless, I have heard many people say they regret working too much instead of attending to the relationships with their loved ones.

Balancing Pitta sleep

It is particularly challenging for too hard-working Pitta people to relax in the evening and do nothing. They might even find relaxing really unpleasant and would rather max all hours of the day. To balance they should try to live by the motto, 'Everything in moderation'. Refraining from working in the evening is imperative while balancing your sleep. High achieving Pitta people dangerously close to burn-out must prioritise finding ways to unwind, or it is only a matter of time before they hit the wall. Avoid intense workout sessions late at night because your sleep is disrupted by the heat of Pitta burning hot at night. Try to find a way of letting go of the 'must do' thoughts and create space to unwind. Perhaps a calm and peaceful evening walk or meditation outside, or in a cool room, will dramatically reduce excessive Pitta energy. Take some time to think about the root of your disrupted sleep. It is advisable to introduce balancing routines in case you experience any further Pitta imbalances, including skin problems, gastritis, stomach ulcers, migraine, inflammation, infection or high blood pressure. The most important measures for balancing overheated Pitta energy is to eat Pitta-balancing foods and learn stress management/conflict resolution.

Summary of tips for stimulating Pitta-sleep

- Refrain from working after dinner in the evening.
- Make time for calm activities, avoid violent films and computer games.
- Set clear targets for how you would like to sleep.
- Take a relaxing evening walk.
- Do not eat anything after your evening meal and only drink cooled down boiled water.
- Go to bed on time in the evenings, not later than 11:00 pm.
- Train yourself to let go of thoughts about work and anything else you would like to plan. To control your thoughts, you will need a few other thought options to actively select between once you 'start work in your

thoughts'. Make a note of any positive and relaxing thoughts you would like to exchange the negative thoughts with.

Kapha sleep disruption

Kapha people usually sleep well as it takes longer for them to succumb to stress and pressure. Their dilemma is that they are able to shift day and night by sleeping later in the morning and go to bed late or very late at night. Those with the most Kapha energy will be most stable and suffer least sleep disruptions. Initially, it is usually people close to them who will be most disturbed by them shifting day for night. Kapha people find it difficult to get up in the morning and often oversleep. As Kapha becomes more imbalanced, the harder it will be to get going in the morning. Frequently, they do not feel awake and ready for the day until lunchtime. Long-term Kapha sleep disruption will sooner or later result in imbalance and consequently disillusion and hopelessness. Kapha-people are those most prone to heavy depression if they do not pay attention to their sleeping habits. They also have a tendency to sleep their troubles away rather than doing what is needed to change their lives to increase vitality. Other signs of Kapha imbalance includes avoiding sorting out a bad relationship, being unhappy at work but not knowing how to change the situation and finding it difficult to muster up the energy to get things done. Kapha imbalance is a sign of inertia, avoidance and stagnation. The theme for balancing Kapha is stimulation based on exercises and getting into a daily rhythm with routines.

Balancing Kapha sleep

Inherently, Kapha people have a passion for a comfortable life, which means that often they will choose a lifestyle giving them short-term satisfaction, commonly involving a lot of good food as well as sleep and only a little physical activity. For Kapha people, their lifestyle always leads to weight gain and eventually to health issues such as depression and food addiction, as well as difficulties putting theory into practice and going after their goals or even being able to determine their life goals. To create balance, Kapha-people will need to correct their sleep rhythm. They actually need the least sleep of all the doshas, therefore I recommend they get to bed by 11 pm and get up no later than $6 - 6.30$ in the morning before the Vata time ends. That way the light energy of Vata will stay with them throughout the morning activities. Kapha people often snore, either due to being overweight or because they sleep too heavily.

Summary of tips for stimulating Kapha sleep

- Set a clear objective for how you would like to feel during the day.
- Make a conscious decision about what time you intend to go to bed and more importantly, what time you want to get up in the morning. Make use of people around you to ensure you definitely get up.
- Go to bed at the same time each night and get up at the same time each morning during the period of time you are balancing your sleep rhythm.
- Do not eat anything after your evening meal and ideally drink some warm boiled water.

- Finish off the evening with a brisk walk.
- Keep to the same sleep rhythm on weekends.
- Establish a morning routine that will get you out of bed in the morning.
- Eat Kapha-balancing foods, see the 'Appetite' chapter.
- Exercise daily.

Long-term sleep disruption

For most people, one of the most effective ways of breaking a spell of bad sleep is to start exercising. Regardless of what we do, trying to find short-cuts through sleeping pills and herbal or other remedies, the fact remains that we are made to move our bodies a lot throughout the day. When we refrain, sooner or later we will all become imbalanced, some quicker than others.

All sleep disturbances do not necessarily imply something is immediately wrong. It might even be the body being given extra time to clear this and that up. For instance, in cases when sleep disturbances stem from a life crisis or traumatic experiences, it may well be that we needed time to reflect. Rather than fighting the sleep disturbance we might as well just accept and get used to it for a period of time. Sometimes however, the sleep problem remains once we have come out the other side of a crisis; that is the time to seek help to get back into a good rhythm.

Some even advocate completely disrupting the sleep cycle in order for the sleep to find its own natural rhythm. The easiest way to do this is by not sleeping at all for a whole night, although you might need help to keep awake. The following day it is important to keep active and not nap at all during the day, as well as staying up until about 10 pm before going to bed. Most people will naturally feel that sleep is imminent and the body is usually exhausted enough that sleep will come quickly. Should the sleep pattern still be disrupted, including waking up several times at night, the same procedure can be carried out during the next 24 hours. Unless the sleep disruption is due to medical reasons, staying awake for 48 hours will generally make most people fall into a natural sleep pattern.

Suppressing emotions is an effective way of inviting sleep disruption, as the feelings will surface at night when the brain is processing emotions, thoughts and impressions. Valuing yourself and your feelings and getting help processing your feelings in order to let go of them, may be necessary for returning to your natural sleep pattern.

Finally, these tips are only recommendations and only you will know when you are rested. That is when you will know that you have found your own natural sleep pattern.

The trick is to become aware of what it is that brings you strength and energy and then dedicate more time to activities enhancing, rather than draining your vitality.

Coaching tips

- *Identify your sleep patterns and any disruptions to your sleep.*
- *How are you in the mornings?*
- *How do you feel when you go to bed? What are your thoughts?*
- *Make a note of what will further improve your sleep.*
- *Focus on your daily rhythm and make a note of what type of rhythm you would prefer, and then compare with the rhythm you are in today.*
- *Prioritise three things you are willing to do to improve your sleep and to increase your vitality.*
- *Keep to these routines for 21 days before evaluating your experience.*
- *Remember that the likelihood of succeeding depends on how clear your resolution to make changes is.*

5

Appetite

" Most people live as if they are going to live forever. I live as if I will die any day soon."

Nikos Kazantazkis, Zorba the Greek

Appetite, feel this word. A word that can arouse many associations within us. Most of the people I coach ask me about food and the most common question is, "What should I eat to stay in balance?"

It certainly is important to think about what you eat, since food is a significant part of what we are made of. It is, however, far more important to start thinking about feelings around food and whether we choose well-prepared nutritious foods from the most natural sources as possible. I always recommend choosing non-toxic, organic and ethically sourced food, as far as possible, because food holds energy in many different ways. We would not want people to suffer just so that we can eat until we are full! Or would we? Something to think about as we generally only associate the energy of food in that which we can see, weigh and measure. I believe there is much more to it than that. Digestion is also affected by how greens have been grown and animals have been cared for. Animals exposed to severe stress before slaughter contain a lot more stress hormones which makes the meat tougher, and consequently we end up ingesting more stress hormones. Many animals are given antibiotics and other medicines that we absorb when we eat the meat. Moreover, the medicines also enter our waterways and pollute the ground water which eventually becomes our drinking water.

Many indigenous cultures, including native Indians and Aboriginals, speak of universal balance. The saying goes that Mother Earth and everything on earth, will treat us the way we treat them. Effectively, this means that if we only see to our short-term needs by using intensive farming methods leading to soil depletion, adding artificial additives to food and treating slaughter animals in an unworthy manner, one way or another, the day when it all backfires on us will certainly come.

The food we eat travels through approximately eight meters of digestive tract, where nutrients are broken down into smaller parts for your body to absorb and use for energy and growing new tissue. In essence, the food is simply transformed into a new part of you. The food you just ate will go through an exceptional process to be digested and broken down, transforming nutrients so that they can absorbed by your body. So, the first question is, how is your digestive process? If in good working order, your body has the best possible chance of keeping you strong and healthy. Your immune system is then intact and able to defend you from internal as well as external threats. Basically, your body is like a house, it will be easy to mend and renovate as long as its foundation is solid and the construction is strong. There will be more work to be done on a house built on a bad foundation. Why not begin building a strong and healthy digestive system straight away? They say, "The way you have taken care of yourself over the last 10 years is the way you feel today. The way you take care of yourself today is the way you will feel in 10 years".

Our five senses are all involved in enhancing our vitality through the food we eat with different hormones aiding, or disrupting, our digestion it is affected by our sight, hearing, taste, touch and smell. The digestion process begins at the sight and smell of good food when saliva is excreted into the mouth, which help start the digestive process. The food is digested and broken down inside the stomach with the help of substances and enzymes produced by hunger. The food continues down via the pyloric sphincter to the first part of the small intestine called the duodenum, also known as the 'intestine of twelve finger-widths' as it is believed to be that long. This is where many different nutrients are absorbed by the blood and transported to, among other areas, the liver. The liver takes care of and deals with the digested food and distributes it to other parts of the body. I call the liver the food distributor because it distributes different substances into the bloodstream and to various other areas of the body. Any remaining digested food, that has not been absorbed by the small intestine, continues through the small intestine and the colon, where the liquid is mostly absorbed. Whatever remains will eventually land in the toilet and provide you with evidence of how well this magnificent process has worked for you.

Most people in our culture are guided by the clock for deciding when to eat, rather than by their hunger signals. This is particularly disadvantageous for Kapha people because that dosha has the greatest tendency toward obesity and being overweight. In ayurvedic practice the digestive fire is called Agni (fire) and how it burns in your digestive system is quite critical to your health. If burning too fast, producing too much Pitta, it will be at risk of burning to the extent that it breaks down the mucus membranes in the intestinal tract causing gastritis, ulcers and inflammations. If burning too slow, the risk is that it is not powerful enough to "burn" the food going through the gastro-intestinal tract properly. Since many of us eat when we are peckish rather than hungry, the digestive fire is not fully ablaze and ready for digesting optimally. According to the ayurvedic knowledge the food will not digest properly if you eat when you are not hungry. Instead it becomes an insufficiently digested food mass called Ama (sludge) which will eventually enter the body and get stuck, often in critical places. The closest reference for understanding Ama from a western medical point of view is arteriosclerosis, or fat deposits and calcification of the blood vessels that, among other things, increasingly produce high blood pressure as the sludge gets stuck inside the blood vessel. Eventually it will cause obstruction of the blood vessel, which means that the blood is not able to move past the clogged area, or ischemic, also known as angina pectoris/cardiovascular disease which occurs when the heart muscle is deprived of oxygen. Cardiovascular disease is still the most common cause of premature death in the western world. From an ayurvedic perspective it is, among other things, due to food we eat not being digested properly and residues of inadequately digested food being absorbed into the bloodstream and sticking to the blood vessel walls. This process creates high blood pressure as undigested food stuff and fats get stuck and narrow the blood vessels. Previously it was believed to be a natural aging process. Unfortunately, it has been found that due to the western food culture, undigested fats/food begin to settle inside the blood vessels from about 10 to 12 years of age and reaches its peak at the end of Pitta time, at 40 to 55 years of age, which is when most cardiovascular diseases occur. To continually feel stressed also creates problems with digestion, as being in stressful situations turns off the digestive process and instead increases the production of stress hormones to help the body survive. To eat while stressed means both that any hunger signals are shut off as well as the stress hormones disrupting the digestive process. Then it does not matter how well the food you eat is prepared, because you will not be able to utilise the nutrition optimally anyway. Occasionally eating while stressed is, however, not a problem. The point I would like to make is that the general lifestyle we have adopted means that we eat on the go and feel pressure to keep up, which will sooner or later create problems for us.

As most diseases are partly caused by bad digestion and most of our common diseases have been shown to be closely related to diet and how we eat and digest food. Only focusing on *what* you eat, and not on *how* you eat, means you have not got the whole point. Numerous studies have shown that people living around the Mediterranean are significantly less affected by cardiovascular diseases, diabetes, obesity and similar issues, than Swedes, for example. It has generally been thought that the reason has been their diet alone and consequently today we import to Sweden and have added many Mediterranean foods such as olive oil, garlic, red wine, fruit and vegetables to our cooking. I would, however, suggest that food is only one part of the understanding of people being healthier in those countries. Their food culture is still different to ours and they view meals as a social setting where you take the time to both enjoy the food as well as the company. Sadly, habits such as siestas are disappearing due to requirements for increased effectiveness which is also influencing the Mediterranean communities.

We may live longer in Sweden than most countries, but we are definitely not particularly healthy during our lifetimes. More than half of the population of Sweden has one or more symptoms of chronic conditions and we pop pills like never before. It is easy to get lost in all the research on how we should live and eat to stay healthy. It is actually not that hard to understand how to eat if we ask ourselves the question; Which types of food are we meant to eat? According to gene researchers, it takes at least 50, 000 years for humans to change their genes. How did we live 50, 000 years ago? We certanly did not have fast food restaurants, 24-hour stores or night shifts! Looking into what is known as evolutionary medicine will provide you with a lot of information. It is a rather new and very exciting research area studying how humans have lived since ancient times, to find out how we, aided by this information, can come to an understanding that can help us live in a more balanced way today. Evolutionary medicine researchers are carrying out studies on people on a similar diet as people during the stone-age, a diet consisting of a mix between vegetables, fruits and nuts along with meat, fish and shellfish. Findings show that these people succumb less to illnesses common in the western world today.

The human race originated in Africa, as we believe, and we began emigrating about 200, 000 years ago. Certain populations adapted to eating more meat, the Samis and the Eskimos for instance, but they still ate what our genes were adapted to. It was not until people became farmers cultivating the soil that we introduced a diet for which we were never really created. Basically, we are not made to eat grains, which became the most common crop, as it belongs to the grass species. Our digestive system is not adapted to break down grasses sufficiently and many people therefore have difficulties digesting grains like flour which contains gluten. It has been discovered that one way to increase the ability to digest grains is to create fermentation processes such as found in sourdough bread, for example. Besides farming we later began keeping cattle and milk increasingly became an integral part of our diet, which had not been part of our natural food tradition from the beginning. Most people lack an important digestive enzyme that breaks down milk proteins, which means that they cannot digest milk and clearly these people should avoid all milk products. Today we eat grains, milk products, excessive fat and unbelievable amounts of sugar together with meat from farm cattle, containing a lot of saturated fatty acids (about 70% fat compared to game at 30%), which means that the body has to work hard taking care of both food foreign to our bodies and breaking down excess proteins, fats and sugar, which we are not made to handle. Together with all the additives, dyes, preservatives and everything else that is currently put into our food, the body has a tough job keeping healthy. Of course, all this can sound really depressing, because how on earth should we eat then to stay in balance? My experience is that anything too complicated will never become a habit, so choose some simple tips to follow if you would like to overhaul your diet in order to increase your well-being.

Now it is time to talk about the odd things!

Begin by observing your digestive functions by also observing your bowel movements. This is a rather sorry story, since a large part of the population has gastro-intestinal problems. It can be a little embarrassing to talk about and is not usually a hot topic of conversation at dinner parties, although anyone who has experienced a stomach that does not function well, knows it is torture. If you are dominated by Vata your stool will tend to resemble rabbit pellets, you may have a lot of gas in your stomach and you can easily become constipated. From an ayurvedic perspective, it is natural to relieve yourself each day. Not having daily bowel movements means that the food starts to decay, more than it should, in the intestines. Constipation is a result of too much Vata that can be due to too much stress, cold food and drink, irregular eating, little water, sleep disorders, worry and anxiety, a lot of travelling or too much physical strain, among other things.

Having mostly Pitta in your constitution, you will have a tendency towards loose stools and if imbalanced, it can be very loose with diahorrea. A strong Pitta imbalance with several bowel movements a day, will make it hard for the intestines to absorb nutrients and you will be at risk of malnutrition. Should you have loose stools mixed with blood your intestines are inflamed. Common Pitta symptoms include acid reflux, gastritis, ulcers, diverticulitis (infected intestinal pockets) and being intensely hungry before meals or feeling hungry soon after a meal. Bad breath is a clear sign that Pitta is imbalanced.

As a rule, the digestion of Kapha people is slow and they usually empty their bowels once a day. Often, it is heavy and they can have a feeling that the bowels have not really emptied properly. The Kapha constitution has the same qualities as Ama (sludge) which makes Kapha people collect sludge easily, usually in the form of fat and excess mucous. Opposed to Pitta people suffering high blood pressure, Kapha people with high blood pressure have generally not got it because of stress; it is more likely due to having collected too much sludge inside their blood vessels which has made the vessels too narrow. As you already have understood, you can have both causes to high blood pressure and all constitutions can succumb to high blood pressure, but some are more predisposed than others.

Balancing your digestive system

1. Eat just three times a day. The most important thing is to make sure you are hungry before meals. Sometimes it is enough to wait a few minutes before you eat if you are not hungry, then the hunger will come. Hunger is the sign that your digestive fire is activated and ready to digest the food that goes down the gastro-intestinal tract. When you start paying attention to your hunger signals you will notice when you become hungry, how often and whether you are hungry in the morning. If you are dominated by Kapha you will discover that your hunger signals are not very strong. My recommendation for you is although I am

now about to tell you something that will make many dieticians hit the roof to eat less for breakfast and even for dinner. The most important thing is to make sure you are really hungry for lunch when the digestive system is the most active during Pitta time in the middle of the day. Always eat a meal prepared well and enjoy it.

Vata people will notice that they cannot eat much at every meal. This means that they will get hungry and their blood pressure will drop easily just 2-3 hours after a meal. For them, I usually recommend eating a snack mid-morning and one in mid-afternoon. Best is to snack on fruit since fruit will be digested directly without going through a major breakdown process, which will ensure you will be hungry at mealtime. Pitta people will notice that their digestive system is strong with very noticeable regular hunger pangs before every meal. Sometimes the hunger pangs are too strong and do not allow time to eat before their mood deteriorates and they become irritated. Make sure to drink cooled boiled water between meals to effectively balance any fluctuation.

2. Do not eat or drink anything between meals other than water, and then preferably boiled water, if you are about to balance eating habits. If you are a more Vata type take a small meal in the afternoon. Constantly ingesting fruit, sweets, sandwiches, coffee, tea, or something else between meals means the gastro-intestinal tract never gets to work in peace and then rest before the next meal. It

takes about four hours to digest a meal and during that time you need to give your body the space to break down and process food without being disturbed or interrupted. Many people eat things without even being conscious of doing it. Food, drink and the mouth are our best sources of comfort, something we learnt when we were given the breast for comfort as babies when we were crying. Vibrant health and a strong immune system begin with our digestion. You can create favourable conditions, with the help of a good digestive system, for your body and mind to optimally handle stress, bacteria, viruses and other disruptions. To develop this power, it is important that you eat only when you are hungry. When you are hungry you can really enjoy food and choose foods you really like. It is important to give yourself the time to enjoy food because then you will develop a host of good pleasure hormones that help to break the food down. Another tip is to never eat less than two hours before bedtime to allow the stomach to break down the food before you go to bed. The evening is Kapha time and everything moves slower, even our digestive system.

Ayurveda and the six flavours

The six flavours in ayurvedic tradition are much more than just flavours. It is the six flavours sweet, salty, sour, spicy, harsh and bitter upon which the entire ayurvedic pharmacology is based. Ayurvedic medicines are based mainly on herbs and spices and the tradition for using these substances and their effects is long. The effect of each herb can be different depending on which constitution you have. Armed with a little understanding around how the flavours affect us, it will be easier for you to create a meal based on your own constitution.

The effects of the flavours

- Sweet increases Kapha but decreases Vata and Pitta. We find it in honey, rice or milk, or a small dessert after a meal.
- Sour increases Pitta and Kapha and decreases Vata. We find it in vinegar, dressing or lemons, as well as sour fruits and vegetables.
- Salt increases Pitta and Kapha and decreases Vata. We can add it when it is not in our food.
- Spicy flavours increase Pitta and Vata and decrease Kapha. We usually add it in the form of spices from pepper, chilli, and ginger, or in spicy raw ingredients like radishes, horseradish, and black radish.
- Harsh increases Vata and decreases Pitta and Kapha. It is a flavour that we do not always think we recognise, but if you have tasted an unripe banana then you will know what I mean. We need a lot less of the harsh flavour and we will find it in beans and lentils, and in green salad that is also bitter.
- Bitter increases Vata and decreases Pitta and Kapha. It is the taste we need the least of to satisfy our needs. We often find it in green leafy vegetables like salad and spinach.

Balanced digestion according to the three constitutions

Vata

Eat breakfast, lunch and dinner. The basis for a Vata breakfast is warm food like porridge or semolina, or nuts and dried fruit cooked with the porridge. Vata people must remember to eat warm cooked food that is more moist than dry. Avoid cold salads and other cold foods such as ice cream, cold yoghurt, especially in the winter which is Vata season. Drink boiled warm water, about 6 to 8 cups by the mouthful throughout the day, preferably also with meals. The warm water brings energy in the form of warmth, helps to cleanse the body and makes sure that Vata people do not become dehydrated. If you suffer chronic constipation, then regularly drinking boiled water throughout the day is a perfect remedy. Also avoid raw salads and too much fibre that absorbs even more water and will make you more constipated. Instead, quickly stir-fry your vegetables in a small amount of fat, which will make them easier to digest. Thin, underweight Vata people can, to their advantage, eat some fatty fish like salmon or some organic meat.

Pitta

Pitta people are recommended to eat three times a day and rarely snack. During summer time a Pitta breakfast consist of yoghurt, sour milk or other cool foods, unless you have Pitta symptoms. Otherwise a fruit salad is recommended as breakfast for sensitive Pitta stomachs. In the winter have warm porridge or, even better quinoa, since it is not a grain. Pitta is the dosha that often has the strongest digestive system and can therefore eat cold foods like cold salads and yoghurt, especially during warm seasons. Choose warm cooked food during the winter seasons if you live in a cold climate.

Pitta should beware of highly spiced food if Pitta symptoms are making themselves known. If you have problems with gastritis, ulcers or skin problems then choose milder foods, reduce all hot, red (Pitta) products such as red tomatoes, red peppers, carrots, chili, red meat, red wine, etc and also reduce intake of sour flavours such as vinegar, orange juice, cheese, etc.

Out of balance, Pitta often gets very strong hunger pangs before meals. If a Pitta person does not eat in time they can get very irritated and angry. A simple way to balance the intense hunger is to drink about 6 to 8 cups of *cooled* boiled water regularly throughout the day. Pitta people can be very thirsty and tend to gulp cold drinks during meals, which increases the risk of extinguishing the digestive fire that is needed to break the food down. Have some water with your meal but drink moderately during meals. Mankind has drunk wine for thousands of years, not just because it tastes good, but also because wine aids digestion. Drinking a glass of wine with food can increase the digestive process, as long as it feels good to you and you can keep to a reasonable amount. Half a bottle at every meal is *not* a reasonable amount! Pitta people are those susceptible to becoming addicted easily in particularly where alcohol is concerned. If you have a tendency towards addiction and are not able to control the amount of alcohol you drink, then of course you must first regain control. Or else you risk the bottle taking control of you. Finally, because Pitta people often are on the run, practice giving your digestion a few minutes to break down the food before you leave the table.

Kapha

Kapha people tend to disrupt any hunger signals as they often eat even when they are not really hungry and easily confuse hunger with cravings. Because Kapha people have the slowest digestive systems it also takes longer between meals for them to become hungry again. Therefore, Kapha people are recommended to pay particular attention to their hunger signals. Their slow digestive systems make it easy for them to gain weight and they are least likely to be hungry in the morning.

From an ayurvedic perspective, breakfast is the least important of the three meals. If you have a heavy Kapha constitution, and are overweight, it may be to your advantage to eat a little less in the morning. During the winter, porridge with fibres, for example buckwheat which is an herb and not a grain, is recommended. For Kapha people it is of utmost importance to make sure to be properly hungry before lunch. Lunch is the time of day mostly influenced by Pitta and most people do naturally feel hungry. Excess weight is treated by increasing the digestive metabolism. To ensure that Ama, or sludge, does not accumulate it is vital to feel hungry before meals.

Kapha people should think about eating a little less for breakfast, lunch and dinner. To speed up your digestion and perhaps lose weight, do not eat anything between these three meals. As Kapha people tend to accumulate a lot of fluids, drink only warm boiled water regularly throughout the day, about six cups maximum. Kapha people should eat fairly dry, hot food, without sauces laden with fat. Eat strong spicy food; ginger is particularly good for increasing the digestive fire.

If there is any constitution that is strongly recommended to reduce meat consumption, it is the overweight Kapha person. If not for ever, then for a period of time. Because meat takes longer to digest than fish and vegetables, reducing your intake of meat for a period of time can help increase your digestive fire. Reduce heavy, fatty and sweet dishes and have more tasty, spicy and light dishes. Water with ginger at every meal will increase the digestive fire. Boil a litre of water, steep with about eight pieces of fresh ginger added, for 5 minutes. Filter and drink hot with food. If you would like to increase your digestion still further, then eat a small piece of fresh ginger 15 to 20 minutes before eating. It is like adding fuel to the fire and most people will become aware of clearer hunger signals before the meal.

More tips for creating vitality with the help of food

- Eat only when you are hungry! If you are not hungry before a meal, try to wait a little while until the hunger signals come.
- Use fresh ingredients as much as possible, avoid processed foods. Everything you eat turns into new tissue so choose fresh produce that you would like to become a new part of you. Personally, I prefer organic, locally produced and natural fresh ingredients.

- If you eat meat, increasingly choose game if you can, or grass-fed meat to reduce the amount of saturated fat you absorb, as the body has a hard time breaking it down.
- Ideally, eat fish and shellfish several times a week because they contain good fats. Make sure that they are ethically sourced and contain as few toxins as possible.
- Try to reduce grains (bread, all flour food, biscuits, etc.) and milk products, especially if your constitution is dominated by Kapha. Those who easily break down milk are Vata and Pitta people, although it can be a problem for Kapha people to digest milk products since they do not have the same capacity to break down the milk. From the ayurvedic perspective people dominated by Kapha are prone to diabetes. Consider that in less than 50 years, Sweden has reached the highest incidence of diabetes in the world. Currently, there are almost 50 million diabetics in India, since the introduction of the western food culture. Swedish children are among the highest consumers of milk in the whole world and milk contains a lot of lactose that the body has to break down. Day care centres that teach children to drink water with their meals help the children create a good habit. Water is what humans have been drinking since time began, even if there are groups of people that both can and do feel good drinking milk. Of course, you should have milk if it makes you feel good, but if you have an imbalance and your constitution is Kapha, I recommend that you try reducing your milk intake.
- Do I need to mention that reducing all sugar intake in the form of sweets and biscuits, soft drinks, etc is important? Our sugar

consumption has never been as extensive as it is today, and consequently diabetes is on the increase. It is common in many cultures to enjoy a sweet something after eating, and it has been found that eating something sweet in connection with a meal, rather than between meals, does not interfere negatively with our blood sugar levels. Ayurvedic tradition recognises that you will leave the table satisfied if your meal has included all six flavours: sweet, salty, sour, spicy, harsh and bitter. Leaving the table without having satisfied all the taste buds leaves you craving something shortly after eating. In fact, we often incorporate the whole range of flavours while cooking, without really thinking about it.

- Do not add too much salt to your food. Although we need salt in our food to break down and assimilate it optimally, unfortunately, most of us ingest more salt than our bodies can handle. Increase your awareness about how much salted food you eat and try to reduce it if it is too much.

- How we perceive digesting the food we eat is more important in Ayurveda than its fat, carbohydrate and protein content. Nutrient absorption will vary for different people based on which constitution they are dominated by and how balanced and effective their digestive system is. If you are lucky enough to have been blessed with a strong and durable Pitta fire within your digestive system, you will be able to eat almost anything you like and still feel great. Should your constitution, on the other hand, be dominated by Vata or Kapha or you have a Pitta imbalance expressing different Pitta symptoms, then it will be to your advantage to start eating a more balanced diet in accordance with your constitution. Trust your sense about what feels good and what does not. Only you can be the judge of what is good for you to eat, although, most of us would benefit from becoming more aware of how the food we eat makes us feel.

- Place a hand on your stomach before your next meal and ask yourself how hungry you are on a scale from 1-6 where: 1 is ravenous; 2 is definitely hungry; 3 is hungry but can wait, 4 is full, 5 is definitely full and 6 is very full. After the meal place your hand on your stomach again and ask yourself how full you are on the same scale. It is good to start eating at 2 and stop at 4.

- Meals are sensory experiences, so if you would like meals to increase your vitality try making them as enjoyable as possible, light a candle, sit down, take time chewing your food as it benefits your digestion, avoid solving family conflicts or work issues during mealtimes. The choice is yours!

- Do not mix cooked and uncooked food. Cooked food has gone through a different breakdown process in the saucepan before landing in your stomach. It is further on in the digestive process than raw food, which will take more effort to digest than cooked food. If you would like to develop a resistant, life affirming digestive system, then you should eat freshly cooked food, as often as possible, with a small salad on the side to introduce harsh flavours to the meal. If included in your meal, make fresh fruit the first part of your meal since it goes through the digestive processes faster than cooked food. In fact, it is actually better to keep fruit as snacks.

- Choose warm cooked food, as and when available, since it is easier for us to digest and assimilate than raw food. Should you be governed mainly by Pitta, the easier it will be to digest uncooked food, and then it is fine to eat. If in the midst of a Pitta summer, or you find yourself in a hot climate, you will discover that eating raw, cold food is not an issue.

- Food contains life force, or Prana, as it is called in Ayurveda. That is what you want a lot of, especially if you are ill, worn out, stressed or exhausted. We get Prana from lovingly grown and gathered food caught and eaten with gratitude and joy. What you do occasionally is not that important, but consider what you do in your daily life because that is the foundation for your wellbeing and what will help you develop vitality for life.

- Drink coffee if it makes you feel good, and if so, at the end of a meal, as coffee, among other things, is harsh and bitter and disrupts digestion needed at the beginning of meals. Harsh and bitter flavours suppress hunger pangs and drinking coffee between meals may put you at risk of not producing strong hunger signals. If you carry excess weight, removing coffee between meals is one of the first things I recommend.

Lastly, some reflections

Consider how you feel after each meal. Do you feel refreshed and alert afterward, that you have eaten food doing you good? If you feel sluggish, tired and bloated, then you should think about how and what you have eaten.

- Dare to break old habits. Eating habits are often inherited and might not be suitable for you. Experiment with food to find out what you like as well as what makes you feel good.
- Pay less attention to all the new recommendations telling us what to eat and start listening more to yourself, and your own stomach, particularly how you feel on the food you eat.
- Be honest with yourself. Take a look at what you look like. Do you need to lose or perhaps gain weight? Food and exercise have always been the way to true health.

Most people keeping to a modern western diet will sooner or later have excess weight issues because most eat too much. Remember that since time began, our bodies were made to digest food two or three, times a day and are not adapted to constantly being fed excess amounts of food, in particular not the amount of fat, sugar and meat we ingest today. Grains are at risk of diminishing our digestive fire (as are all foods foreign to our bodies or that which we over consume). As mentioned previously, studying populations still living as we did in time immemorial, we can see that these folk groups rarely or never succumb to illness!

Many common diseases are a result of our lifestyle, food habits and lack of exercise. By looking into what we need to survive and comparing that with how we live today, it is easy to understand the difficulties the body will experience, attempting to keep in balance during a whole lifetime. You would probably think it crazy to give elephants cream cakes and sweets. Why? Because they were not created to digest that. Neither are human beings, but we still think it is perfectly fine to eat this type of food. Wild mammals are usually effectively free of disease. When people adopt animals as pets, they also fall ill when given food they are not created to digest.

Summing up when it comes to food, it is pointless making our life too complicated or it will not work. We can simply follow two rules:

1.   Pay attention to hunger signals.

2.   Eat food that is as natural as possible and pay attention to what it is that makes you feel good.

Coaching tips

- *Begin eating according to your circadian rhythm; breakfast between 6 and 8 am, lunch between 11 and 12 am and dinner between 6 and 8 pm.*
- *Drink warm boiled water regularly, or cooled boiled water if you are mostly Pitta or experience Pitta symptoms, about 6 to 8 cups by the mouthful throughout the whole day, 6 cups for anyone dominated by Kapha.*
- *Raise your awareness about hunger and fullness signals by placing a hand on your stomach before you begin eating to determine what hunger level you are at. Repeat after meals to determine how full you are. Stop eating at around 4.*

- *When you have followed the above for two weeks you can begin to create meals based on your own constitution.*
- *Vata - hot cooked meals with sauce, somewhat heavier (especially in the winter) and nourishing.*
- *Pitta - hot cooked meals, avoiding strong spices, remember everything in moderation and eat just enough, that is to say, stop eating before you are too full.*
- *Kapha - hot cooked meals with less sauce and somewhat drier fresh ingredients.*

6

Stress, crisis and joyfulness

"Don't be afraid to scream. It will free your mind of sorrowful thoughts."

Hopi proverb

Today, we know all too well that stress makes us sick. Around 30 years ago stress and burnout were becoming hot topics. Burnout Syndrome, however, was nothing new. It had been on the radar for several years in the US where research into what it actually entails had come far. Professor Christina Maslash and her colleagues at Berkley University in California had identified burnout syndrome in the 70s and found that it was often highly educated people and those working with people in health care, schools or social welfare, who mainly succumbed to burnout syndrome. How times have changed.

We now live in a society which reveres highly developed social skills. Since relationships and networking are the most important tools in our private and working lives, more people than ever before need advanced social skills. Space to be left alone, being quiet, introspective and slow is diminishing. We are in constant communication with others, on our mobile phones, via the internet or in physical meetings, which leads to increased demands to handle ever more relationships than before. At the same time, we are expected to be more and more independent and make more individual decisions about our lives. While enjoying the individual freedom we have attained in our part of the world, each and every one of us needs to learn how to handle that independence, including setting healthy boundaries. Contemporary people must adjust to receiving an ever-increasing amount of impressions faster, as well as making decisions faster. Stress ensues when there is imbalance between the expectations on an individual and what the person can live up to.

When I began studying other cultures and meeting people with experience of meditation, tai chi, yoga, prayer, qi gong, and other forms of contemplative and conscious-raising activities, I realised that such activities had existed in all cultures, to teach people to cope with excessive stress and pressure, something all societies have been forced to do from time to time. Natural disasters, war, hunger and hardship have always been around, and the capacity of human beings to adjust and handle their situations is unique. The question is, how do we move forward from here? Children who have grown up during the last 20 years belong to what I refer to as "the hurry up generation". They have constantly heard their parents telling them to "hurry up". How will they turn out as adults?

In the last two decades, women have increasingly demanded, and to a certain degree achieved, more independence through education. For example, more women enter higher education than men these days, although many women sense they are expected to be homemakers, secure and calm, and be there for their children, while at the same time climbing the career ladder and keeping themselves attractive and fit. In the wake of increased equality, the level of stress has also equalled out, and reached a new peak for fathers of young children who are much more involved in the care of their families than men of previous generations.

Prioritising may be the most important skill for anyone living with prolonged stress. We cannot do everything, always, and always perfectly. However, stress is not just about performance, stress can also stem from feeling abandoned, excluded, not feeling involved and loved. The feeling of not belonging is devastating and from a public health perspective, loneliness is the most urgent problem in the western world. Loneliness and exclusion are a breeding ground for issues such as, smoking, addiction, inactivity, bad food habits, drugs and criminality are just a few issues associated with loneliness. In many big cities in the western world, 60 to 70% of households are single households. When will we see new meeting places being developed which could help alleviate loneliness?

Still, I believe positive changes have come with the progress. I think most people enjoy their independence and feel that they do not have to follow a certain path decided by their family and relatives. Instead we can, underpinned by our freedom, initiate meetings which will develop new types of social structures, which is already happening. The numerous networks popping up are proof that we want to find new social settings for interacting.

What exactly is stress?

Stress is based on an idea that something is stressful. The thought can be conscious or subconscious. All signals reaching our five senses are interpreted by the cerebrum which if interpreting the impression as stress, immediately sends signals to the hypothalamus. The hypothalamus, located in the centre of the brain, is often referred to as "The Board" for the body and keeps track of most processes in our bodies, such as temperature, blood pressure, pH-balance in the blood and many other things. It forwards signals to the pituitary gland which is a small hormonal gland situated right below the hypothalamus. The pituitary gland can simply be called "The Managing Director" of the body that implements and makes sure things happen, which, in turn, sends signals to the other hormonal glands; thyroid, adrenal, ovary and the testicle glands. The level the stress hormones, adrenaline, noradrenaline and cortisol, which are excreted differ depending on how we are affected by stress. All the hormones moving around in the body affect all organs and the nervous system. Positive high-performance activities such as sports, for example, mean that it is mostly the adrenaline and noradrenaline levels that are increased in the bloodstream, while negative high-performance activities, such as rushing around at work and never being able to catch up, increases the cortisol production as well. It is believed that cortisol increases the negative effects of stress as the blood flow becomes slow and the risk of plaque clogging the arteries increases and the blood pressure being elevated as a result. Cortisol also affects our digestive fire, decreasing our capacity to digest well, which as you already have become aware of means that our ability to digest food is reduced under stress.

Simply put, the nervous system is divided into two parts. One part is consciously controlled by will. Basically, if you think you want to bend your arm, you will bend your arm. You control the movement by your thoughts. We also have the autonomous nervous system which is the nervous system in charge of making sure all bodily functions work without us having to consciously think about them such as: heart beat frequency, blood pressure, body temperature, blood pH-balance, and a host of other processes. The autonomous nervous system is the part we can affect through enhancing our awareness, for example, while meditating, doing yoga or other conscious enhancing activities.

The sympathetic nervous system	The parasympathetic nervous system
"The Accelerator"	**"The Brake"**
- heart beats faster	- heart beats slower
- breathing accelerates	- breathing slows down
- large muscle groups receive more blood	- blood collects in the stomach and in the small capillaries, among other places, in the fingers and toes
- digestion deteriorates	- digestion improves

| - Stored energy is released | - the body stores energy |
| - catabolic, breakdown effect on the body and mind | - anabolic, developing effect on the body and mind |

The autonomous nervous system is divided into two parts. One is called the sympathetic nervous system and is often referred to as the "The Accelerator", which represents energy-enhancing processes initiated in conjunction with increased performance and stress. The other part of the autonomous nervous system is called the parasympathetic nervous system and is generally called "The Brake" and is the part of the nervous system that represents peaceful and calm feelings inside the body. As stress increases we increasingly lose control over ourselves, our behaviour and our thoughts. While stressed, we become inefficient, make more mistakes and create more conflicts. Basically, it is an ineffective way of working and living.

Everyday life means creating a balance between the two nervous systems. When one is switched on, the other is switched off. While exercising, the sympathetic nervous system is turned on and a catabolic process is initiated in the body, which is great if we do not exercise too hard, or for too long. While exercising, cells are broken down and dispersed into the body and later when we relax and are satisfied, the anabolic effect increases and produces new cells. To stay in balance and reach your full potential, you need to move your body *every day* to remove old waste products so that new strong tissues can be made. With the help of exercise, stress and tension stuck in the mind and muscles leave the body, which allows the parasympathetic nervous system to develop.

Find the appropriate exercise for you to achieve balance based on your particular pre-conditions. Find mentors, instructors, coaches, attend fitness classes, start your own groups, walk or, even better, jog together with dogs and friends, find new ways of being more active. Exercising is definitely one of the most important factors we all have for enhancing our life force, and there is an abundance of positive effects to gain. Once again, remember that it takes 21 days to change a habit. Get started today, do not mull it over and, especially, do not evaluate before 21 days have passed. That is when you can ask yourself if you feel better, worse, or the same as before, and decide how to continue.

To fully understand stress, it is important to realise that historically, we have an innate capacity to handle stress. The problem is not stress in itself. The issue is that as long as the sympathetic nervous system is turned on, the breakdown process continues. Eventually, the body is not able to maintain balance. You have probably already realised that the more stress and pressure you expose yourself to, irrespective of whether you experience the stress as positive or negative, the more you must compensate by relaxing, in order for the parasympathetic nervous system to restore the energy you have expended. Otherwise all your reserves will be depleted. I call this the knowledge of 'The First Rule of Life' skills. If you have learnt to relax between highly demanding and stressful periods, you can still live a good life without running the risk of being exposed to harmful stress. Successful people in high positions within politics and the business community know this, as do both male and female top athletes. Those who are successful have mastered the art of balancing and being in control of their lives and set time aside between highly demanding and stressful periods to ensure they relax.

So, how do we know when we have achieved balance? Well, that is highly individual and related to our constitution, current state, age, gender, etc. The easiest way to find out is to listen to what your body is trying to tell you. If you are very tense, you will have various symptoms that you might recognize, and you will know when your basic tension is low, as you will feel relaxed, both mentally and physically.

Signs of high basic tension

Stiff all over

Irritation

Shoulder pain

Difficulty concentrating

Headache

Restlessness

Heart palpitations

Forgetfulness

Shortness of breath

Poor sleep

Stomach problems

Depression

Infections

High blood pressure

Signs of low basic tension

Flexible body

Patience, tolerance

Relaxed shoulders

Good concentration

Lots of energy

Increased capacity

Stronger immune system

Good sleep

Buffer against stress

Stable mood

Crisis

When we face a crisis, are forced into change or exposed to
excessive stress, we generally also lose the ability to manage our
lives constructively. If what we are going through is serious and
threatens our whole existence, we will feel scared and vulnerable
and our behaviour can be described based on what happens to most
of us when facing a crisis. Reaction to a crisis follows a certain
pattern, even if the length of time it takes to go through the full
process differs. Denial about what has happened is commonly the
first reaction. This is a completely natural reaction that helps us
handle difficult information. By the time we acknowledge that what
happened, has actually happened, most of us start feeling enraged
and angry. After a while we grieve and feel fearful and, finally,
when we realise that things will never be the same as before,
resignation. Eventually, we will inevitably have to make a choice
between either losing our spark totally, becoming bitter and
disappointed in life, or we make the decision to move forward. It is
when we feel it the most, when we are just about to give up, that
somehow life forces us to be brave, and after all, move forward and
defy the pain. Slowly, we stumble forward and reach the deal-
breaker, and stop fighting for what we cannot have and accept that
things will never be like they were before. If we succeed, we will
reach a place of acceptance and then seriously be ready to take full
responsibility for our progress again. It is only when we have let go
of being defensive and given up accusing any external or internal
circumstances for our pain and the awful situation we are in, that we

are in a position to move on. It is only then that we are open to actively reaching out for help.

Everyone faces crises at one time or another. After a crisis, most people realise that life will never be the same and gain a better understanding about the nature of life being unpredictable. This insight is painful to accept, but if we are ready to accept the fact that life is constantly changing, we can carefully take steps toward a future that we cannot always predict. In time, we are hopefully able to let go of the darkness and the chains around an illusion of how things should be that have held us back. Once through the crisis, we are ready to rethink our reality and gradually see that there are other ways to live life than the way we lived before the crisis. Most people I have had the honour of supporting through a crisis, confirm this point and often say afterwards that "without this crisis I would not be the person I am today". Essentially, they have a feeling of having gained something, despite the process often taking a long time and being painful. Life suddenly becomes richer and more colourful, and the drudgery of daily life before has suddenly become a source of well-being.

The problem is not that human beings are exposed to crises, but that we have not been taught that they are part of life and what to do when we end up in one. Stress, crises, broken illusions and troubled love lives, are all part of life. It is just that this particular lesson was not on the agenda when we went to school. We have never really been taught anything about the rollercoaster of life, so when life is turned upside down we are totally unprepared. Everyone has, or will, experience a broken heart, death, disease, debt, conflict, loneliness, meaninglessness and other afflictions in life. The clever thing is that we actually are created to get through these situations. Humankind would not have survived if we did not have powerful resources within us, to get us through incomprehensible crises. We have an enormous ability and potential to get through difficult situations, if we just get support from people around us. As fellow human beings, we can become what I call 'living crutches', for people in distress for a period of time, while they get through their crisis. Care for and ask your friend how they are, if you become aware that someone you know is going through a crisis.

Unfortunately, we are not that easy to help when we have entered the darkness. We are tired, despondent, angry, sad, depressed, and we sulk and prefer to dwell on, and go through, our problems time and again, which is when we need someone who has the energy to listen to us. Keep listening. Next time it might be you who needs to dwell. Dwelling is a part of the process and we need to understand and confirm that our feelings are acceptable before we can let them go.

All of us can practice becoming more resilient in life and personally I believe finding purpose in life is part of the equation. The concept of the Sense of Coherence coined by Antonovsky about having a purpose in life making humans more resilient during difficult times. The more difficulties we have in grasping the purpose, the more difficult it will be to endure a crisis. When Nelson Mandela was asked how he coped for 27 years behind bars, he said it was not about coping. He only saw two options, either wither and die, or prepare for the day he would be released. He kept preparing himself for 27 years! The ANC and his fight against apartheid gave him a purpose.

Start by asking yourself the following questions:

- What do I find meaningful?

- What am I prepared to fight for?

- What is most important in my life?

- When do I set boundaries for what I am prepared to do?

- How far am I prepared to go before saying no?

- What do I need to initiate changes now?

- What am I waiting for?

The anatomy of joyfulness

If stress can break us, the power to restore us must also exist. There is a lot of information about the negative effects of stress but not as much about the results of passion and joy. That we feel better when we are happy is obvious and something you will believe without any heavy scientific evidence. There is a saying that goes "Whether you think you can or cannot, you are right". This means that what you think, will also become your reality. To believe that we have the power and energy to get us through hard times, increases our potential of doing just that. The more power you put into your decision to choose to see possibilities, rather than obstacles, the more likely you will be to succeed.

An American pharmacology researcher named Candace Pert has done research in the area of psychoneuroimmunology. Her research shows clearly that thoughts steer our physical processes. Human beings are made up of billions of cells and we are controlled by the hormones produced in our bodies. Which hormones are produced is dependent on which thoughts we choose to think. Depending on the thoughts being pleasurable or unpleasant, the sympathetic or the parasympathetic nervous system will be activated. Each cell is equipped with its own intelligence, and decides which substances to allow in and which to block, in order to function. As hormones and other substances are released into the bloodstream, they will reach cells which are covered by a membrane. For the substance to enter the cell, the cell must produce receptors that work as keyholes so that the substance can squeeze through the membrane and into the cell. Depending on which substance that is in the blood, the cell adapts and produces appropriate receptors accordingly. When a lot of stress hormones are present, the cell produces a lot of stress receptors which allows the cell to let in substances that can instigate stress in the cell.

Pert's research shows that we can become addicted to our emotions in the same way as a heroin addict can become addicted to heroin. The numerous receptors around a heroin addict's cells scream for more heroin if they do not get any once the receptors become depleted. If the cell does not receive any heroin, it will start breaking down and the heroin addict will go into severe withdrawal. The same applies to our thoughts. During prolonged stress, the body reacts by increasing the production of stress hormones. When they arrive at the cells, they reciprocate by increasing the production of the corresponding receptors. Once through a stressful period, the receptors still hang around the cell, which will make us go into withdrawal, and experience discomfort, restlessness and inner stress, which we may find hard to define. To satisfy the cell´s need for stress hormones, subconsciously we stay in the stress or hopelessness phase, to provide the cells with the substance for which they have developed receptors.

It is time-consuming to revert this process, which can be viewed as scientific evidence for ayurvedic tradition suggesting it takes 21 days to change a habit. When initiating change, at first you must tap into your will power. During this period of time you should simply make the decision to implement whatever it is you have decided upon without letting your internal saboteur take over, since that is just your old pattern of behaviour trying to play a trick on you. As it happens, in the same way that cells can become dependent on stress and discomfort, it has been shown that cells can also become dependent on pleasure and joy, and even become immune to displeasure and stress. Research on Buddhist monks who have lived for a very, very, long time with peace in their hearts and minds and practiced meditation for an extended period of time, has shown they are missing the ability to feel stress and displeasure. Maybe that would be utopia in our daily life, but science shows that how we choose to interpret reality and how we relate to it, is what will decide if our daily lives will strengthen us or break us down. Capturing constructive and hopeful thoughts and repeating them when things are not going your way, is the way to conquer freedom of thought and your own vitality.

We react differently to stress

Everyone reacts differently to stress and displeasure. Our tenacity differs and we have all been through different experiences which have affected us. We are also armed with different circumstances for working through past stressful experiences which will affect how tolerant we are, as and when we encounter the next stressful issue. Consequently, our stress tolerance levels differ, depending on for instance daily fitness regimes, age, gender, family situation, social network, education, earlier experiences, health and constitution. We will all be equipped with different life skills.

Vata

Vata people are the frailest and often react early to stress and pressure and tend to be self-destructive during severe stress. Vata people are driven by the wish to please people and want to be liked by those around them. That is why they go to great lengths to adapt themselves in different ways. Therefore, they do not set clear boundaries to maintain their integrity and easily become turncoats. As things move faster and faster, quicker decisions will also need to be made. Vata people tend to worry about making the "right" decision, which often leaves them agonising over decisions. They keep worrying that they have made the wrong decision and that others will not agree with them. They easily lose control and increasingly become controlled by their emotions. The stress increases in step with worry and anxiety, and if the destructive pressure does not abate, panic will always hover just below the surface. Vata people often question themselves and easily lose their self-confidence, since they do not really trust their own power, as they feel very powerless when stressed. Vata people are sensitive to the ebb and flow of stress symptoms and pain, mood swings, worry, cramps, constipation and headaches are all typical Vata symptoms which will move closer and closer to the surface.

The most common stress reactions of Vata people

Emotional reactions:	*Physical reactions:*
Scattered	Constipation
Worried/Nervous	Dry skin and dry hair
Scared of making mistakes	Loss of appetite
Superficial	Back and neck pain
Sleep disorders	Headache
Anxiety	Cold
Burnout because of hopelessness	Cramps
Collapse	Tremors/Shaking
Medicine/drug abuse	Hypotension

The stress reactions of Vata people tend to be self-destructive and they blame themselves more than others for their failures. They can sink into deep despair and totally lose their self-esteem and lose faith in their internal resources. Communication skills during stress quickly deteriorate and become incoherent for Vata people and when exposed to very high stress levels they can become hysterical and start screaming.

Pitta

Pitta people are driven by a strong will power and can therefore withstand a lot of pressure before admitting they are stressed. They enjoy and are attracted to challenges involving a certain amount of stress. Once they have carried on until they have sacrificed remaining in balance, usually they will initially notice that they are losing concentration and they start taking their irritation out on others. It is obvious to people around them when a Pitta person is experiencing stress, they can both see and feel it. Frustration and anger always hover beneath the surface even if not all Pitta people express those feelings at first. Exposed to too much stress, they might lose control and become angry. Generally, they become imbalanced due to time pressure in combination with far too many demands, and they may feel that others stand in the way of their decisions. Pitta people are often highly confident and clearly express what they feel and think and their integrity is also intact. The more stressed they become, the less likely they are to compromise. They have a tendency, during highly stressful times, to view the world as black or white, often believing that they are right.

Should they find themselves in a really pressured situation, they would walk over bodies to win. Obvious Pitta symptoms include heat, skin problems that come and go, gastritis, ulcers, fever, inflammation and high blood pressure.

The most common stress reactions of Pitta people

Emotional reactions:	*Physical reactions:*
Lack of concentration	Skin problems
Irritation	Irritated eyes
Anger	Gastritis
Temperamental	Stomach ulcers
Burnout due to time pressure	Severe headaches
Alcohol abuse	High blood pressure
Cynical	Cardiovascular problems
Manipulative	Inflammation

Pitta people tend to become more destructive toward others during stressful periods. If they become too out of balance, they may become violent and aggressive, both towards themselves but mostly towards others. The greatest weakness for Pitta people is their hot temper which will constantly need balancing. While exposed to high stress levels, Pitta people communicate clearly, raise their voice, point with their whole hand and clearly articulate how far others can go.

Kapha

Kapha people are stable, slow and live more comfortable lives, seldom exposing themselves to high stress or pressure. They rarely enjoy big challenges, and they prefer to stay on the side-lines and watch. They generally choose contexts where they can be more methodical, and they like to take one thing at a time. Kapha people are inherently calm and have the capacity to avoid getting worked up unnecessarily. Yet, if they do get stressed out, they will find the situation very uncomfortable and become even more quiet and introverted. They may find it hard to express their emotions, not because they do not want to talk about them, but because they may find it difficult to identify them. They tend to become indecisive and withdrawn when stressed, often they isolate themselves and avoid social contact because it is often people who make them stressed. Large gatherings can induce stress and they often hang around reflecting for a while before they enter a new situation. They will recognise stress symptoms such as being tongue-tied and irresolute because they need time to reflect, having a sense of inertia and not being able to get to the point. A sense of stuckness and feeling unable to change the situation, are both signs of Kapha out of balance. It is usually Kapha people who are the closest to abusing food through perpetual comfort eating. When they fall into a destructive mindset they easily end up in deep depression and inactivity. They have the ability to sleep off difficult and troublesome feelings, instead of talking about them, and they risk becoming bitter unless they get help to let go of old issues.

The most common stress reactions of Kapha people

Mental reactions:	*Physical reactions:*
Introverted	Heaviness
Restrained	Overweight
Quiet	Blocked up nose and throat
Blocked emotions	Sinusitis
Tired and heavy	Dull ache in the body
Depression	Stiffness
Bitter	Swollen joints
Eating disorders	Nausea

Kapha people are more self-destructive when they are out of balance and they are often reluctant to seek help, consequently a long time may pass before they admit that they are unwell and need to rest. They sacrifice themselves a lot for others, but at the risk of becoming bitter when what they believe they deserve is not reciprocated.

Balance during stress and pressure

In order to balance life to increase vitality, it is important that we know what to do to be in charge of ourselves. Being guided by our emotions is not always constructive, especially when we end up in stressful situations. Creating opportunities for reflection is one of the most important and successful tools that I teach for handling stress. Unless you first become aware of what is actually happening and what you would want to happen, it is hard to follow any advice at all. Based on the information about the three constitutions, there are some simple tricks that you can utilise.

Vata

The more stress and pressure a Vata person are exposed to in life, the more important it is to relax and take it easy, or else life will spin out of control. Turn off the computer and the telephone, and reduce all external impressions to a minimum in your free time. If you need to restore strength, take a warm shower, or even better, a warm bath. Take the time to oil your whole body with sesame oil and it is particularly beneficial to massage oil into your scalp and ears as well as your feet, since they contain many nerve receptors which you can calm down through massage. Drink warm boiled water, or if you like milk, drink boiled warm milk with a little honey and saffron in it (remember that sweet flavours decrease Vata). I suggest that you do not add the honey to the milk before it is cooled, as honey leaves residues when it is heated. During stressful periods it is even more important for you to follow your daily routines and be sure that you sleep well. When Vata people get caught up in work they can "forget" to eat and neglecting food is a sure way of quickly getting out of balance, so set your alarm and eat at regular times. Yoga, meditation, qi gong or other quiet and calm activities are really good ways for regaining balance. By doing a short and simple session in the morning, you will have created a buffer for any stress you might encounter during the day. Beware of exercising too hard during highly stressful times and listen to calming music in the evenings to recover instead of watching TV, which tends to increase our inner stress.

Pitta

Once a Pitta person begins to become increasingly critical and frustrated, it is time to stop before your body tips you over. Dare to believe that in fact you are not irreplaceable and that others can watch things while you take a break. Dare to let others take more responsibility and learn to delegate more. Relax and release through activities not requiring you to achieve anything. Listen to music, take walks through beautiful areas, sit in a greenhouse and meditate, go to the theatre. Simply let others take care of any chores and let yourself enjoy just being. Meditation is a great way to let go of the constant need to be busy all the time. The need to relax for Pitta people who have endured a lot of stress over a long period of time is usually huge, since they are constantly driven to outdo themselves. Women, especially, need to beware of their perfectionist side so that it does not become destructive. Keep to the motto "good enough" in your everyday life. Work enough, exercise enough, drink enough and eat enough. Cool yourself, and your heated emotions, down with a cool shower in the morning, eat cool and mild food, drink cooled boiled water and oil your body with cooling Pitta oil in the morning after your shower. Put time aside in your calendar for reflection to ensure you have regular meetings with yourself, preferably in a beautiful environment. Make sure that you go to bed on time during periods of high stress and pressure and, above all, make sure that you sleep during Pitta time, between 22 - 02. Should you need to be efficient and increase the waking hours of the day, wake up earlier in the morning instead of staying up late at night.

Kapha

When Kapha people realise that they are stuck or have stagnated and become introverted, instead of tackling what is making them feel stressed, it is time to get a grip in order to not get stuck in a deep Kapha imbalance. Get exercising as a matter of urgency and make sure you get sweaty when you exercise. Set a clear goal for what it is you want to change. Make a solid decision once you have decided to create more balance in your life and create a structure for your daily routines which you will follow to a fault for 21 days. Make sure you get up before 6.30 and start the day by doing a short exercise session. Do some gentle stretches, even if only for just a few minutes. Distinguish a few different activities that you would like to accomplish that are both fun and educational. Challenge yourself to try new activities that you have not done before. The more overweight you are, the stricter you must be with food and exercise and only eat three times each day. Make a schedule and involve your friends or family in the changes you are making, so that they can help and support you. Perhaps you will need someone that persistently tells you each and every day that you must get moving and get off the starting blocks. If you do not have anyone close by, I do recommend that you write clear notes about your plans and stick them on your bathroom mirror, your fridge, in your office. Kapha people easily fall into the habit of saying "put off today what you can do tomorrow", which makes tomorrow full of things that have been put off and eventually become too much to handle.

Coaching tips

- *Define what currently makes you stressed and write down the five biggest obstacles for why you are not in perfect balance.*
- *Write down how you would want to feel when you are in balance.*
- *Write down five things you need to be balanced in order of priority.*
- *Choose the three most important things and plan for how you will implement them.*
- *Involve people around you, friends, family, colleagues, who you know will support you.*
- *Tell your "coach" about the changes you intend to make over the next 21 days, ask him/her to ask you each day how things are going.*
- *After 21 days evaluate how things have been, celebrate things that have gone well, if need be adjust your routines and continue for another 21 days.*

7

Personal development

"The ability to think differently today than yesterday, distinguishes the wise from the stubborn."

J. Steinbeck

Every one of us has skills strengths and talents. There is not even one person who is not talented at something. It is just that we have not always found our strengths and some of us are particularly good at hiding them. Some of us tell ourselves that we are not good enough, that we are not adequate, that perhaps we do not have the right to be part of what is good in life. Far too many of us also waste the skills and strengths that we actually do have, by not utilising them to the fullest. The majority of the people I coach and support have developed one, or perhaps two, of their skills. The truth is that we all possess a number of skills concealed within us, ready and waiting to emerge and take shape. Sometimes it is hard to acknowledge your strengths because what we are good at is so simple to do and it is easy to fall into the trap of believing that it is just as simple for everyone else. Your skills, which are easy, simple and effective and not a struggle at all for you to apply, are unique to you. Honestly, do you believe that we were born to utilise just a fraction of our potential? Or to be bitter, disappointed and feeling victimized?

Almost all of us have at some time or other throughout our lifetime been in a slump and wondered what the point was of carrying on, struggling through this thing called life. In the end, it turned out that it was that dip and its darkness that eventually gave us a new perspective on life. The insight might even have helped us understand that nobody will thank us for, making ourselves appear smaller than we really are. It is not about being better than anyone else, it is about applying our unique powers at 100%. Nobody else would judge us the way we judge ourselves. Listen to your internal voice for a moment. Would you ever accept your friends talking about you in this way, the way we carry on speaking to ourselves day in, day out? *How will things work out for you really? Can't you do better than this? Who do you think you are? Why do you think you will succeed? Who is really interested in hearing what you have to say? Go faster! Hurry up, you have to do more! Run faster! You don't have time! You're too fat! You're too skinny! Your look is all wrong!*

What will happen if we pay attention to these thoughts 24/7? Right answer, lack of energy. We know this, yet it seems we are stuck in a pattern that has shaped us since childhood. I cannot say this enough, only that what we give our focus to will prosper. By perpetually repeating negative and low energy messages internally, our lives will become a self-fulfilling prophecy. Many of us have assumed that we are never good enough just the way we are and believe that if only things were different, then life would be better. A better husband, a better wife, nicer children, a new job, more money, bigger breasts, a smaller nose. We constantly target things that need fixing before we can allow ourselves to believe that we can feel good and even be happy, believing that happiness is out of reach and not something to accompany us in our everyday lives. This becomes very clear to anyone being told the illness they have been diagnosed with is terminal. You would think that having received such news that you would want to seize the moment and tick off things on your bucket list, visiting exotic places, going on adventures, but most people just want to live longer and take advantage of the small moments in life. Throughout life we spend more time trying to fix our weaknesses instead of developing our skills. The incredible story below is proof of unbelievable strength hidden within.

This story is about an Indian woman, Muda Erraka, who is illiterate, poor and lives in a particularly poor area of India. It was a challenge for the women in her village to collect water each day. They had to walk far to fetch the water, which was of poor quality, and she didn't have any means of supporting herself. One day the village was contacted by a charity whose goal was to eradicate poverty in India, but since the Indian woman believed she didn't have anything to offer, she didn't go to the village hall to attend any of the meetings. One day after the other women asked her to come to a meeting, she appeared at the meeting, and before long she suddenly found herself taking the initiative to fight for bringing water to the village. The process was long and arduous, but she never gave up. In the end she was the woman whose unrelenting determination finally achieved the goal of bringing clean water to her village.

Later she was invited to New York to accept a significant prize for her efforts and her fight. She told her story and how she never ever would have believed that she, who couldn't even read or write and hardly had enough food each day, would be able to fulfil such a dream. A dream she had shared with many others. These women have finally realised that limits are often only a figment of our own imagination.

What might we be able to accomplish, if we brought our powers and dreams to the surface? Why not change to more constructive thoughts like: *If you can, so can I! If I don't know how to, I can learn! Things resolve themselves along the way! I have the strengths and skills to succeed! I am prepared to continue until I succeed! I have the courage to ask for forgiveness! I have a lot of time!*

Constantly being fed misery via newspapers and on the TV does not help us release the power within. We would benefit from hearing many more stories of people making a difference for themselves and others, every single day. Just like the lady in India, we all have the ability to make a difference in our daily life. Someone said, "If you want to be successful, surround yourself with successful people". I have spent time thinking about what success really means, since I, like many with me have connected success with financial prosperity, but have come to realise that this is just one part. Successful are those who, despite opposition from themselves, friends and family, despite the fears, have nevertheless been brave and tenacious enough to continue to believe in and hold onto their dreams, until they succeeded in making them come true. Financial success often follows suit and only those without dreams and vision remain poor.

Not thinking about how we want to live our lives and spending more time being dissatisfied with it, probably means we experience life as a struggle. Sometimes life provides us with time to reflect, a period of time I refer to as "the interim", a period of time for being in the now without having to move forward. If we just hurry through life without stopping and reflecting over what it is that we are striving for, we are at risk of waking up one day wondering what we have done with our lives. "Is this all there was to it?", you might ask yourself one day.

I rarely see businesses, through my work with organisations, departments and managers, who have not set clear goals. For the employees to feel meaningful, be motivated and have job satisfaction, they must find a link between their own goals and what is expected of them at work. Only then will the company grow, and the same applies outside of work. How would you know which direction to take in life, if you do not know the destination? Also, what do you usually do to celebrate your victories when you reach your goals?

Viktor Frankl, an Austrian physician who was incarcerated in a concentration camp for many years during the Second World War, said that it is each and everyone's responsibility to find purpose in life. He believed that we cannot just sit around waiting for life to become meaningful, we have to make life meaningful ourselves.

We must consciously ascertain what it is we find meaningful, in order to enhance our own life force. Should we have had the misfortune of being on the receiving end of too much misery in life such as divorce, loved ones dying, illness, tax debts, not finding love, being unable to lose weight, missed pay rises, deferred promotions, etc then we only have two options for resolving the situation:

1. Change our situation.

2. Change our perception about our situation.

Actually, we have one more option:

3. Refuse to accept our situation and do nothing about it, or even worse; feel that we *cannot* do anything about our situation, leaving us feeling like victims of the circumstances.

If you go for the third alternative it is only a matter of time until you are super stressed and burnt out. As you can see, that option will take you nowhere, a blind alley most of us have been down. Keeping your life force brimming each day is not something that just happens, it is a conscious decision. Symbolically, we must make sure we put ourselves in the driver's seat on this journey called life. If we are not in the passenger seat someone else will navigate our life for us, including our circumstances, relations and the least useful thoughts we have about ourselves. It is time to watch out when we say that we have been "victims" of something, as that effectively means that we have climbed out of the driver's seat and into the passenger seat, which will make it seem as though someone else is driving our life right down the drain. Besides running the risk of becoming angry, sad, bitter, unfairly treated, cynical, revengeful or resigned in these types of situations, we also risk allowing any negative feelings to linger. How inspiring will we then be to those around us? Not at all, in fact those close to us will conform to our miserable demeanour and confirm our illusion about life.

Well, *I am* a victim, you may say! That might be true, but how do thoughts like that help you? Basically, they do not, and the only way we have of relieving ourselves of stress, discomfort, worry, anxiety, fear and despair is to challenge ourselves to take full responsibility for our own lives. The life you desire could be yours, although it will not be easy nor painless. With strong conviction and hard work, it is absolutely possible. If you really want to, invest your power and use the skills and strengths unique to you, and you will become a more successful person, physically, mentally, spiritually and materially. Before our life force can be boosted, we must first accept our situation just the way it is. I might be miserable thanks to someone else, but no one else is responsible for making me feel better, happier or healthier. Once we take on board that we are in charge of our own happiness, we finally understand that it is pointless waiting for someone else to sort our life out. Being part of an understanding and supportive community is a big bonus and should that not be the case, we must find more supportive and inspiring people to spend time with.

Our awareness can be symbolised by an iceberg which can look really small above the surface and still be huge below the surface. Our conscious self is the small part of the iceberg seen above the water surface while our subconscious is the massive part below the surface. Which part of our consciousness, do you think, guide us on a daily basis? The conscious or the subconscious part of ourselves? You guessed it right; it is the subconscious part and it represents about 80% of our total consciousness. This means that most thoughts, feelings and behaviours are instinctive reactions to how we choose to interpret our environment, conscious or unconscious, where patterns and structures remaining from previous experiences continue to control our lives. The only thing you can actually control is what you are aware of.

Our conscious self

Our subconscious self

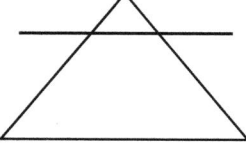

To break negative patterns and instead start developing our skills and strengths, we must introduce more of that which gives us positive power and energy. The first step is to increase your awareness about yourself. The majority of those I coach, including company leaders, students, the self-employed, adolescents, managers, sports men and women, are instinctively unwilling to take a good look at themselves and their own behaviour. Perhaps because we are afraid of losing face, or even our identity, if we discover our "true" selves. This may be the way; discovering that we put a spanner in the works for ourselves and sometimes for others, can often be painful. All of a sudden, we become aware that it is not us deciding what we really want, it is our reflexes governing how we react. Your success, whether it involves building a career to be healthier, serve others, raise children, enhance sports results it always begins with acknowledging that what you are currently doing is what is preventing you from achieving your dreams. My view on personal development includes becoming more self-aware, understanding how we think, feel and act, but also increasing our awareness of how others perceive us and react to how we conduct ourselves.

Listen carefully to your internal dialogue on repeat. What are you telling yourself? Whose thoughts do you carry with you? Are they really yours or might they be a reflection of what people around you expect of you? The brain is very complex but also very simple and only does what we tell it to do. If we tell ourselves, "*I don't have time*" the brain will send that message out into our whole body and your whole being will start behaving as if you do not have time. That is why changing a certain behaviour always begins by altering one belief. To master the art of changing a negative, or not wholly constructive, belief for one that will empower, provide you with more energy and has potential to make you successful, you will need to keep practicing. Otherwise, before long your brain will be crowded with thoughts that will drain your energy. It is important to understand that the life we live is created by the way we think. What I mean is, our life is a reflection of our internal self. To instigate change in your external circumstances, to receive more love in your life, better and more enjoyable jobs, more money, friends, etc, you must always begin by first changing your beliefs. Commonly, we expect change to occur first, before we change ourselves. Nothing could be more untrue. If you want to be happy, you first need to create happiness in your mind, so that you are receptive to happiness. Happiness lives next door, you just need to invite it in.

Obstacles

Why are our lives not a reflection of the amazing qualities we all actually possess? What is it that stands in our way? We have all met or heard of people who, following difficult experiences or crises, have turned things around into fantastic success. It is not as if they have become someone else. That fantastic person was there below the surface the whole time. It is not until we are up against it, that we find ourselves having to choose between darkness and light and when most people realise that it is not worth dedicating their life to living in darkness. All of us find obstacles limiting our potential of living life with a brimming life force. Which obstacles are your favourites? When I lecture, I usually ask my audience about their three most common obstacles for not changing their situation. I have heard all kinds of alternatives. Do you recognise any of these: *I don't have time! I have no money! I can't! I don't want to! I'm unprepared! The children need me! My partner doesn't want to! It seems hard! I might get worse if I try! You know what you have but not what you'll get! Others will laugh at me! I'm too old!* And so on. Can you believe how skilled we are at finding excuses for not taking control of what we really need to change, in order to become more empowered and have more energy in our lives.

Each time change is forced on us, we will perceive the change negatively if it is outside our comfort zone. Most of us need to practice turning negative and energy draining patterns and beliefs into beliefs that provide us with energy as well as constructive thoughts and behaviours. Adopting such beliefs will move us forward and give us the courage and power to choose to go through life with access to all our skills and strengths. One thing is for sure, you have not yet fully developed your strengths and skills. It is never too late to grow and there are no circumstances that cannot be improved. The story below about Jonas shows that we have far more opportunities to create an abundant life than we might think.

Jonas Helgesson was born with cerebral palsy. He was born with the umbilical cord wrapped four times around his neck which deprived him of oxygen. The doctors thought he would not survive but as by a miracle, he did. As a result, however the brain injury prevents him moving the majority of his body as he would like to. His body lives a life of its own with involuntary movements (spasms), stiff fine motor skills and impaired speech. During his childhood he was in a wheelchair and attempts to walk usually did not go well. He kept falling, broke his arms, got blood all over his clothes, and so on. He required a lot of help as well as many aids and it was not until he was 10 years old that he could finally say sentences that others were able to understand. He had custom-made chairs, utensils, mugs, braces for his legs, etc. When he reached teenage hood, life became really tough and there were times when he wondered whether he would have the energy to continue his life.

With a lot of practice, resilience and motivation he became more and more independent and eventually he didn't need his assistant anymore. He learned how to ride a moped and he realised that he was the master of his own destiny. He made the impossible possible even though at times he had to struggle. He decided to live life without making excuses. In his own words, "I stopped feeling sorry for myself and let go of blaming any uphill battles in life on my disability". Today Jonas is a successful lecturer, stand-up comedian, journalist and author. He ends one of his articles with these words: "People with disabilities, like everyone else, think about the future, dream and have ambitions. They also want to succeed in life. They also want to feel that they develop, despite going at a different speed sometimes".

Personal development can be painful. Sometimes it hurts to grow and change perspective. It is even worse when our dreams and visions crash land. Having to come to terms with the fact that something we have believed in is not viable, brings disappointment, grief and despair. Generally speaking, we do not often change the course of our life until it hits rock bottom. Usually we hang on for as long as possible in the hope that life will spontaneously change by itself, which is unlikely to happen until we change our attitude to life.

To have the courage to grow is the greatest gift we can give ourselves, as it can be a really scary thing to do. We tend to hold on to our old, ingrained patterns that prevent us from moving forward. Like being stuck to a ball and chain, to succeed in breaking destructive patterns and commit to go all out for what it is we want, we will need to put all our effort into it. Personal development is not a cosy course where our pain is acknowledged, as that would not help us move forward. You know that you are developing if you find yourself in what I tend to refer to as the discomfort zone. To remain within our comfort zone, without being challenged, means that we keep to our ingrained patterns. To constantly be in the discomfort zone burns us out. Personal development is about taking on small, bigger or huge challenges in life, based on our particular circumstances, skills and strengths. Whether that involves one person beginning to exercise once a week, another aiming to become really good at their sport or someone else winning an Olympic medal, is irrelevant because you should only ever compare yourself to yourself and the results you want to achieve. Taking full responsibility for your own life is to take on board that we cannot change anyone else and that they will only change once they are ready to. You are only responsible for your own development.

Should you be stuck in a situation in which others will be affected by your development, however you will need to consider your options. You must be prepared for any fallout, once you have finally made up your mind to change, even the pain which inevitably follows closely when making changes and taking more responsibility for your own life. At the end of the day, undertaking personal development is not a guarantee for encountering fewer issues in life, rather it will highlight genuine issues and empower us to get them sorted out more quickly. Basically, the more problems we solve, the more problems will come our way. Life will immediately become easier if we acknowledge that problems, or challenges as we might want to refer to them, will always exist and be a part of our life until we die. Problems are gifts in life signifying we are alive and taking part in life. The problem is that we consider problems to be a problem! Accepting that issues and challenges are a part of life will put us in a position of not being surprised the next time they show up.

Ayurvedic psychology

Personal development is, from an ayurvedic perspective, considered something that goes hand in hand with creating lifelong well-being and seen as a natural part of the process of life. That people evolve is a natural process, just as seeds sprout, germinate and flourish. Maturing, not just physically but also existentially, is an innate progress. Now that you have read the book this far, you have realised that a lot of other people, despite their behaviour not closely resembling yours, have a similar constitutional mix of Vata, Pitta and Kapha as yourself. Ayurveda, through the three concepts of Sattva, Rajas and Tamas, exist in everything and are involved in our psyche too, and also takes our existential maturity into account. Just like Vata, Pitta and Kapha, these three attributes also occur together in various combinations.

Sattva is Sanskrit for light and represents awareness and purity, as well as our development which moves us forward. Being Sattvic means to be at peace with yourself and the route to enjoying a more Sattvic life is through awareness, acceptance and forgiveness.

Rajas means movement and represent activity and change. It is the power that keeps the fire burning and makes us brave enough to leap into change and progress. Without Rajas we stand still. Rajas is necessary for creativity and development.

Tamas means inactivity and represents a dark, stationary and retaining power. Tamas is the energy that makes us stop, reflect and create ways to let things die within us, leaving space for the new to come into our lives.

All three attributes have natural functions in this dance called life. Without the movement and change of Raja we will never reach Sattva and a life with internal peace and balance. Without the restraint and stillness of Tamas, we would not notice what rankles with us and what we must do to move on in life. Having Rajas in excess, probably means that life is turbulent, filled with activities and very hectic. Too much Tamas will make us feel we are in the dark, that we are stuck and cannot get things done. The journey through life can be perceived as a spiral where, for every insight we conquer, our Sattva, our internal peace, will be boosted. In order to progress, something that will make us react and change is needed, which is what Rajas represents. Lastly, Tamas stands for broken illusions and brings us grief and pain, which no life can be without.

Tamas is what will make us be more emphatic and humbler towards other people and life in general.

Sattva, Rajas and Tamas in the three constitutions

While establishing the constitutions earlier, we looked at our physical and psychological fundamentals. To come to a deeper understanding of ourselves and our behaviour, it is important to consider our mental awareness, by exploring our maturity in relation to the three constitutions, Vata, Pitta and Kapha. Circle the five foremost characteristics you see in yourself when you are in balance and empowered. Then, circle the five most prominent characteristics you are aware of adopting when entering your discomfort zone and things do not go your way. If you would like to gain even more insight into yourself, let a few people you trust help you by also making a list and compare to check if their perception of you matches your own.

Vata mental orientation

Sattvic:	Energetic, adaptable, flexible, quick perception, good communicator, very compassionate, strong healing abilities, true enthusiasm, positive energy, good starter, good capacity for handling changes.
Rajasic:	Indecisive, unreliable, disruptive, hyperactive, rebellious, restless, nervous, anxious, loquacious, superficial, noisy, interrupts, false enthusiasm, fake.

Tamasic: Victim, scared, inferior, dishonest, depressed,
            self-destructive, drug abuser, prone to sexual
            deviance, mentally disturbed, suicidal.

Pitta mental orientation

Sattvic: Intelligent, clear, attentive, enlightened, role
            model, independent, warm, kind, brave,
            counsellor and mentor

Rajasic: Stubborn, impulsive, judgmental, ambitious,
            aggressive, controlling, critical, dominating,
            nonchalant, manipulative, angry, irate, ruthless,
            proud, conceited.

Tamasic: Tyrannical, hateful, violent, revengeful,
            alcoholic, destructive, psychopath, criminal.

Kapha mental orientation

Sattvic: Calm, peaceful, satisfied, stable, persevering,
            loyal, loving, compassionate, forgiving, patient,
            faithful, nurturing, supportive, trustworthy.

Rajasic: Excessively helpful, controlling, dependent,
            miserly, materialistic, sentimental, needs security,
            seeks comfort.

Tamasic: Numb, self-righteous, lazy, apathetic, ruthless,
            sluggish, greedy, mean, eating disorders.

Now think about which five characteristics you would like to have more of in your life. Write them down. Also, write down how you will feel when you have achieved more of these qualities in your life.

You will discover, once you start paying attention to your own as well as other people's behaviour, that based on the Ayurvedic profiles, we are all more or less predisposed to certain characteristics and behaviours. We recognise what is the easiest for us to do and what strengths we possess and which we do not. It does not necessarily mean that what we are not good at our weaknesses. All it means is that perhaps we should not put in too much effort to become accomplished in those particular skill sets, since that is not where our talents lie. We cannot be good at everything, but we can definitely excel in skills we are strong and talented in.

In order to live our life to our full potential, defining in which parts of our life we feel powerful and avoiding situations we feel powerless, is a must. It will not help, no matter how hard we try to reduce symptoms, unless we implement changes to draining situations that sap our energy, or it will be like having a piece of gravel in your shoe. You can put a plaster on to protect your foot from getting sore, but unless you remove the gravel, it will slowly rub away the plaster and eventually you will have to resort to even stronger means to avoid a wound developing. A life held together by plasters is not a fun life and it does not have to be like that. It is up to you!

Creating balance

Would it not be great if there was a universal solution for how we can become happier and live lives with more vitality? Having said that, I am not going to offer you *one* single solution because there are many different ways to enhance your life force. Just as many as there are people in the world. There are in fact some things we can all benefit from when we decide to steer our lives towards more success in life. For instance, gradually and consciously choosing Sattvic things, environments and behaviours more often, will effortlessly bring you closer to balance and vitality. Indeed, you yourself are best suited for defining what is Sattvic for you, in essence it is whatever helps you evolve long term.

Here are some examples of Rajas, Sattva and Tamas:

	Rajas	Sattva	Tamas
Food	Freshly cooked	Spicy and grilled	Leftovers
Personal	Clean	Smell bad	Dirty and care worn
Behaviour	Understanding	Conflict	Ignorant
Thoughts	Forgiving	Revengeful	Resigned
Work	Creative	Time pressure	Lazy and slack
Activity	Meditation	Hard exercise	Inactive
Circadian	Sleeps at night	Stays up after midnight	Switches day/night rhythm

Self-esteem	Strong	Self-centred	Victim
Confidence	Develops skills	Know it all	Lack of self confidence
Social	Loving community	Community based on status	Isolated
Environment	Recycling	Consumerism	Wasteful

Because we are affected by everything, our thoughts, behaviour, food, environment, etc, it is worthwhile beginning to pay attention to the choices you make. If you would like to increase your vitality, the trick is to include as much Sattva in your life as possible, which is what recharges our batteries, makes space for good thoughts to help us develop, nutritious food for energy, caring companionship and a sustainable work situation. The concept of Ojas, which essentially means life force, is referred to within Ayurveda, and can also be translated to 'the elixir of life'. According to ayurvedic tradition, it is formed in our bodies and minds when we introduce more Sattva in our lives. Keeping our Ojas levels topped up ensures the immune system is strong, protects us against stress, makes us patient and allows us to eat and digest just about anything. A person rich in Ojas automatically attracts many people and it is not unusual for people in general to easily become inspired and get a sense of power from anyone radiating such strong, humble aura and charisma.

A way forward

If you find yourself being stuck in a life situation draining your life force, then it is time to make some changes. There is a way forward even if you have lost your job, gone through a painful divorce, been seriously ill or become disillusioned about a loving and happy life. Should you be lucky enough to be in an understanding environment it will be easier. If not, you need to find people who can act as your role models and inspire you. Most important is that you have made the decision to initiate change, a prerequisite for empowering yourself to avoid anything you no longer want in your life. That enables you to create the space to invite in that which you would like more of. Irrespective of whether it is love, comfort, money, a career, zest for life, fitness, friends, good health or faith, everything begins with a clear and defined decision. The decision involves you having to decline anything you no longer want in your life. Only you can take responsibility for setting your own boundaries.

The ground we stand on today can be fragile depending on what we bring with us from our childhood. Growing up rarely being acknowledged or appreciated can give us a filter through which we see the world. If we are fortunate having grown up in a loving environment, being appreciated for who we are, we will view life differently. Our needs and expectations today are based on how we were treated as children. If you kept hearing that you were only good as long as you were productive, that side of your personality will probably become highly developed. While being told you are incompetent as a child, may lead you to develop that side of your personality, or you may constantly over-compensate the traits you

175

believe are not good enough. All of us, no matter how we grew up, and I really mean everyone, has strengths and skills that we can develop. It is never too late! Below you will find some keys to support you.

Stop fighting. Give up, you do not have to prove anything and this is where your development starts. While struggling we are not able to make any constructive decisions and our perspective on life may also become limited when everything revolves around winning or retreating. Lurking in the background will always be fear and in some cases even terror. For instance, elite sports people know that if their will is too strong, they risk losing focus if they let their will take over. Rather it is all about allowing ourselves to go with the flow, when we are brave enough to fully believe in ourselves and know that we are good enough just the way we are.

Allow yourself to feel disappointment, anger, sorrow and despair. We cannot control our feelings. We can, however, control which thoughts we want to think, but before we can move on, we need to express our feelings. It is also important that our feelings are acknowledged without being questioned as suppressed feelings tend to keep wearing us down mentally and emotionally. Eventually, they will flare up during the next crisis or they will make us ill. Suppressed feelings can be likened to actively trying to push blown up balloons below the surface of the water. As soon as we lose control of any one of them, they will be forced above the surface.

Fully accept your current situation. Your potential for change begins with acknowledging and accepting the current situation. You are in this situation because you have been part of getting yourself to this stage. Everything is as it should be. Nothing can be undone and you cannot change anything that has happened in the past. Open your eyes and evaluate the current situation. See it as it is, not worse than it is.

Find new perspectives of your situation. There are more than 7 billion people in the world and more perspectives on life than yours. Challenge yourself to take a proper look at your situation through other people's eyes, in particular those who might be worse off than you. If that means your illusion of how things are changes, then you are on the right path. Illusions are preconceived ideas of how we think things must be in order to have a happy life, ideas we have absorbed from our environment and upbringing. We must challenge ourselves to think new and different thoughts and hanging on to illusions is not particularly helpful.

Write down what you do not want in life. Initially it is often easier for us to express what we are *not* comfortable with, what we *do not* like and what drains our energy. It might be people, environments or situations, or even our own thoughts and behaviours. Keep adding to the list and then prioritise the three most important things that you must expose yourself to less often, in order to minimise the risk of draining your energy and power.

Write down what you want more of in your life. Doing this is not always obvious for many people I coach. They have a clearer idea about what they do not want and find it harder to express what they really want 100 % more of in their lives, which is the heart of the matter. Many of my clients, both teams and individuals that I coach, do not put enough energy into clarifying what they aspire to. What you wish for should raise your heartbeat while still being achievable. The saying goes, "Reach for the stars and you will hit the moon". In essence, most of us dream far too modest dreams. We tend to settle for less, not believing that we can outperform ourselves and being afraid of the accountability success might bring. It is not uncommon that fears might surface around daring to believe we are successful and able to live up to this image. Trust that you possess the skillset required to take you where you want to be in life.

Write down your plans to take you there. You will not reach your goal without a plan. To create change and achieve success, we need to know how and what we must do. Change jobs or stay in a job, talk in confidence with a friend, ask for forgiveness, start exercising, stop drinking, play more with the children, start practicing being more positive and appreciative of ourselves, our children or partner. Only you will know what must be done to reach your goal. It is your life and surely you are worth success, happiness and love?

Take action. Of course, it is essential to plan and create a structure for what you want to achieve, but without actually *doing* things differently in your life, nothing will happen. Prioritise the most important issue and start making a difference. Take steps toward what you truly need to create vitality and success in your life. When we are broken, destructive and lacking energy, we are of no use either to ourselves, or people close to us, whether it is our children, partner, colleagues or friends.

Get help! Use your friends, family or get a skilled coach who does not say what you want to hear, who will tell you what you need to hear, to help you succeed. Change is often easy as long as it is within your comfort zone. It is only when we reach what I describe as our discomfort zone, that we start to question if we should really go on, if this is the right path. Hold on and keep going. It is now when you should ask people around you for help. Have the courage to believe in yourself, dare to see your success and keep your vision alive each day.

Celebrate your small and big successes along the way. Unless you reward yourself for your successes, things will begin to feel hopeless. Nobody has the stamina or the strength to struggle continuously, so find ways to celebrate, ideally together with others. Be a little crazy, make room for laughter, above all be brave enough to laugh at yourself. Energy and the power to go on can also be found in acknowledging any "failures" if viewed as proof of having taken on the challenge of following our dreams and going for what we believe in. Generally, successful people are not any more talented than anyone else. What they are good at, however, is being brave enough to try, and fail, enough times for them to eventually learn how to become more successful at whatever it is that they are doing.

Having a sense of coherence, from Aron Atonovsky´s research which I mentioned earlier, leads to a strong conviction and belief, so that the foundation for our life will keep us standing when life is rocky. Kjell Kallenberg, a hospital priest and researcher, has supported many people going through crises. He has conducted research to establish whether people who strongly believe in God would stand a better chance of handling and getting through the crisis of a close relative dying, than non-believers. His study shows that people who believe in a forgiving and loving God were supported by their belief going through difficult times, while those believing in a judgmental and harsh God, were not helped by their belief. Daring to ponder the meaning of life, testing ourselves and our own existential and spiritual conceptions, can provide a way to come to an understanding of our own beliefs about what life really is about. The benefits observed by people who have developed their spirituality is that it gives them comfort that everything in life cannot be controlled. That everything is as it should be, even if it is painful at times, accepting that change is part of life, it involves pain as well as joy. That it is essential to take advantage of the beautiful in life, as it could easily be lost tomorrow. Believing is similar to the question about the pessimist and the optimist, regardless of who is right: who has lived the happiest life? A powerful way of implementing positive changes is through ceremonies. Through my work supporting people in attaining their goals, I provide different tools that they can use in their everyday lives. Check out the example in the coaching box below.

Coaching tips

- *Make a Vision plan by writing down what you wish for. Write as if everything has already been achieved. Focus on the areas in your life you want to improve; life, family, relationships, finances, health, career, love, internal satisfaction, etc.*
  You decide how many areas you want to include in your vision for the future.
- *Find a beautiful, appealing stone that easily fits in the palm of your hand.*
- *When you feel that your Vision plan is complete, spend 10 minutes meditating on it. Then take your stone and blow your vision into the stone to "charge" it with the dreams you would like to fulfil.*
- *The trick now is not forcing anything to reach your vision, but inviting effortless change instead. By reading through your Vision plan each morning and ideally before meditating, you will charge the plan with more energy subconsciously and consciously, steering toward the goals you have set.*
- *Bring your stone on your life journey. Each time you squeeze it you will charge yourself with the power and energy that moves you forward.*

8.

Relationships

"Grief shared is half sorrow, joy shared is double joy."

Winnie the Pooh

My conviction is that well-being and harmony begin inside us and are expressed through our relationships. We first emerge through relating with others. By looking at your relationships you will understand more about yourself. What type of people do you surround yourself with? Do they support you? Do you support them? Do you feel energised in their presence? What kind of energy do they absorb when spending time with you? What feelings do you emit? Do you energise or drain people of energy when you spend time with them? Perhaps you are not aware of how you are perceived by others? Many people talk about energy without close consideration as to what that means. Yet, without a doubt, everyone gives off and receives energy, indeed, we even exchange energy with each other despite never having met. The energetic bond in certain relationships is stronger than in others, such as those with our mother, father, children, relatives, close friends and colleagues. In fact, the concept of energy can be found in many different contexts. The food we eat can give us energy, love and physical contact give us energy, our surroundings, the weather and essentially everything in the environment will energise or drain us, in one way or another.

Based on the ayurvedic knowledge of Vata, Pitta, Kapha as well as Sattva, Rajas and Tamas, you now know how to describe the ways different things affect us. In Western culture, we have adopted the belief that we are only affected by things we can see and measure, which is different to the Ayurvedic perception which maintain that many different things, including non-tangible things, affect us despite not being measurable. You are guided through life by your emotions. Your decisions, many vital, stem from your emotions. When did we learn and spend time practicing understanding our feelings and how to handle our emotions? Have you ever been taught which signals to listen to and which you should ignore? Probably not, not in a structured way, at school or elsewhere. The same applies to food, it is more important to experience our perception of it. Some relationships allow us to grow and vitalise us, while bad relationships drain us and potentially even make us ill. The ayurvedic belief is that different constitutions are more or less suited to each other.

It is understandable that a Vata person, whose need for change and flexibility is generally fairly high, having a relationship and living with a Kapha person who craves stability and everything in moderation, will experience a lot of strain in the relationship unless they accept each other's differences.

A relationship between a Pitta person living with another Pitta person can potentially be filled with conflict, should the mental constitution of each be dominated by Rajas. Having more Sattva, they would be better equipped to support each other.

A Pitta person cohabiting with a Kapha or Vata person must always be mindful of the strong energy they emit, as Pitta has the strongest energy that affects other people the most.

Partners can complement each other in relationships, if the other person possesses traits we are missing or have less of ourselves. These traits are often the ones we eventually end up getting annoyed by in our partner. If we meet a person who is more similar to ourselves two Vata, two Pitta or two Kapha people then we confirm our similarities. Since we are also affected by the energies Sattva, Rajas and Tamas in relationships, they will determine how the relationship will develop. Similar to our own personal development between Sattva (insights, understanding and forgiveness), Rajas (ability to affect, create change and stand up for our cause), and Tamas (reflection, stagnation and sluggishness), relationships must also go through all the different phases in order to grow, mature and develop. Rajas in excess, including perpetual disagreements and conflicts, will sooner or later make the relationship hostile and difficult to rescue. If Tamas is excessive in a relationship, lacking change, effort or movement, the risk is that it will come to a standstill. A Sattvic relationship is based on the balance between Sattva, Rajas and Tamas, and is continuously maintained and developed. Without effort, all relationships will wither. We can force ourselves to stay in a relationship, but we cannot be forced to love someone.

Imbalanced relationships

We live in a time of relationships failing like never before and it is becoming increasingly difficult to maintain lifelong relationships, which might be the price we have to pay for preserving our individual freedom. The more independent we become, the harder it is to stay in unfulfilling relationships. So, what is it we want and look for in relationships with others? Since all of us have our own internal strengths and weaknesses, it is likely we are looking to meet people who support and acknowledge our strengths, who will allow us to prosper, as well compensate for our weaknesses, and make us stronger together than we would be on our own. We look to fill the hollow spaces inside us representing whatever it is we are missing. If we have not been seen and heard in earlier relationships with our mother, father and loved ones, the likelihood of seeking out relationships that compensate for what we are missing is very high. The risk of using relationships to compensate for our internal hollowness and shortcomings, is that the burden of filling the empty spaces can become unreasonably heavy for the other person. The more I expect of the other person, without changing myself and mastering these traits in myself, the more likely it is that I am longing for someone who can provide what I never received as a child.

The American psychologist George Peck, says that in healthy relationships two people do not have to be together in order to compensate for each other's shortcomings, they are two people who choose to be together. Essentially, we cannot just *be* in a relationship without continuously working on keeping it harmonic, dynamic and mutually satisfactory, or else it will eventually end. Unless the energies match each other in a relationship, it will just wither. Relationships in which one partner often takes the victim role while the other increasingly takes on the role of being strong, will only work as long as neither change their role. Should the victim personality pick themselves up and start taking care of themselves, the likelihood of wanting to be controlled by, or continuing to receive 'help' from their partner would be very slim. On the other hand, when a strong and over protective partner lacks someone to care for, the risk is that they will feel abandoned and become bitter. By equivalent energies I do not mean that we will never be dependent on the other during certain periods of time in life, rather that the balance between what we take and what we give should be equal over time.

Have you ever tried to change someone else? Then you will know that it is practically impossible, since we are all so different with different needs and ideas of how to create balance and well-being. Many people who come to see me ask about their relationships. Usually it is about a partner or children, and why they do things in a certain way and not the way that would be the most natural way to the person asking. Understanding the different constitutions will help you to appreciate that living with a partner, children or friends of a different constitution to you, will mean that they have different needs and habits.

There is a concept for describing the "dance" we all enter once we begin to relate to someone else. The model is called "Karpman's Drama Triangle" and it stems from Transactional Analysis, a psychotherapy method founded by Eric Berne in the 1950s. The model was conceived by Stephen Karpman, an American psychiatrist, and describes the human interaction we are all involved in, i.e., how we relate and communicate with each other. The Drama Triangle is an aid to explain how we repeatedly, consciously or subconsciously, keep searching for a position in relation to other people and includes three characteristics referred to as:

- **Persecutor:** anyone striving for power, influence and control of others who uses their strength and aggressiveness to influence others.
- **Rescuer:** anyone being acknowledged as being a perpetual rescuer, who will help others without first having been asked and controls others through caring.
- **Victim:** anyone who abdicates responsibility by constantly needing someone else to take care of and help them, who manipulates others by being helpless and dependent.

Karpman´s Drama Triangle – being imbalanced

We participate in this type of role-play with virtually everyone we meet and usually we do it unintentionally. In any given situation, we automatically strive to find our spot in the triangle. The role we play may differ depending on who it is we are relating to, be it our boss, mother, father, children, a customer, our partner, etc. Irrespective of who it is, we, deliberately or automatically find our position in the relationship. The more destructive the relationship, the more likely we are to adapt to the role play described in the Drama Triangle. If you find yourself in a relationship with someone who mostly takes on the role of being a "Victim", it is highly likely that you prefer being a "Rescuer", because you will then be provided with a "Victim" to take care of, which is what a "Rescuer" needs in order to feel seen and heard. Should your partner decline your suggestions or does not follow your advice, you may lose patience and switch and become a "Persecutor" loudly expressing your opinions. The "Victim" may also become frustrated and take on the role of "Persecutor" too. Two people cannot be in the same position at the same time, therefore a power struggle ensues for the position whereby one "wins" the position and the other has to move on to a different position.

We carry on like this, usually completely unaware. What we can do is to try to become more aware of which role we tend to take on most often. A "Rescuer" does not like to ask for help and will therefore, for as long as possible, avoid admitting their weaknesses to themselves or others. A "Persecutor" may want to be perceived as a "Rescuer" and will try to take that position, but just until their patience runs out and if it serves their purpose. Once they have reached their stress limit, they will fall back into the "Persecutor" role and go into battle. Anyone taking on the "Victim" role will also have abdicated responsibility of their own fate, and needs a "Rescuer" to take care of them or a "Persecutor" to order them about. The "Persecutor" desires a "Victim" to control and consequently they are often in relationships with a partner they can dominate. Incidentally, this is exactly what the "Rescuer" wants too, ensuring they always have someone to help and support.

Nobody stays in the same position all the time, each day we all shuffle around in the array of different roles. Now that you have become aware that we are all different and are governed by different constitutions, you will notice that Vata, Pitta and Kapha people are inherently drawn to certain roles.

Pitta people, with their strong energy and expressive temperament, have a dominant trait and often end up in the role of the "Persecutor" when imbalanced.

Kapha people, who feel acknowledged by always putting themselves in the "Rescuer" role, will patiently clench their jaws and offer help despite not being asked and generally strive for the role of being the "Rescuer".

Vata people, whose self-esteem is often fragile, feel helpless and delicate and often seek the "Victim" role.

Consider which roles you are most comfortable in. Also, think about which roles you fall into automatically when you find yourself in your discomfort zone in times of stress and discomfort. Explore which roles you feel most resistance towards. This will probably be your biggest challenge as well as your greatest opportunity for personal development. Always falling into being the "Rescuer" may indicate that you find it difficult to set boundaries towards other people and you will constantly be there more for others than yourself, which will expose you to feeling that you are being taken advantage of. Consequently, you may become bitter towards those you try to help who might not show enough appreciation for the help they receive.

If you are adverse to the "Persecutor" role, perhaps you need to take on this role to learn to set healthy boundaries, find your integrity and the courage to say no. If, on the other hand, you usually find yourself being a "Persecutor" who knows it all, you will probably have a hard time putting yourself in the "Victim" role and risk feeling vulnerable, exposed and emotional. Being vulnerable opens up the opportunity for a "Persecutor" to understand and discover their own shortcomings and potentially make them more humble and emphatic.

In turn, the "Victim" goes through life in pain feeling exposed and does not have the courage to trust their own strength and potential. The "Victim" learned early on that they are not good enough, feeling excluded and have been holding on to this belief ever since. The "Victim" has the potential of realising how powerful they are and start making their own decisions. The power lies in discovering the "Persecutor" within and begin to take control of themselves and their own lives, and no longer let themselves be controlled or dominated by someone else.

Considering where we fit in amongst the different roles has the potential to enhance our awareness of how we relate to other people, and think about which traits we hide, and which ones we reveal. Neither role is "right" or "wrong", the point is to gain insight into the consequences of our interaction with other people. Being successful on a personal level is different for all of us. Being successful might involve creating the consequences we would prefer in our relationships with other people and in different circumstances. Paying attention to, and above all, being open to receiving feedback of how other people perceive us, is key for anyone wanting to build healthy relationships.

Pitta people have a lot of charisma and with it, dominant traits they need to be mindful of as they tend to become dominant in relationships. That's what Pippi Longstocking says: "If you're very, very strong, you must be very, very kind!" The Pitta person's strength of character and energy are their most important assets. Vata people are more fragile and sensitive, and their strength and assets allow them to contribute with creativity, change and openness in relationships, while Kapha people are more supportive, stable and take time for reflection, which is their strength as they contribute with care, thoughtfulness and calmness in relationships.

For every negative behavioural trait there is a positive, although as mentioned earlier, we are generally quicker to point out our weaknesses than acknowledge our strengths. If you are aware of the 10 weakest behavioural traits in yourself, you can then look at them from a different angle and ask yourself what strengths are concealed behind the weaknesses. True success, to my mind, is about being in a position to help others increase their vitality. By increasing our awareness of the mark we leave on the people we meet, we can gear the choices we make towards building healthier relationships. This means that we must have the courage to pay close attention to how we behave ourselves, particularly when we are going through a rough patch. The further off balance we are, the less we will be able to control our own behaviour. We cannot actually control and govern anyone else's behaviour, only our own behaviour and how we react to our feelings and thoughts.

Most of us live a life full of stress, pressure and internal conflicts, which from time to time will rock our centre and as a result, the relationships we have with other people. By scrutinising our stress patterns, we can gain insight into what behavioural traits we would like to change to promote harmony in our relationships, whether it is with ourselves, a colleague, a partner or any other relationships. It is easy to fall into the trap of believing that the problem is external, rather than anything to do with ourselves, when we find ourselves in difficult situations and think it might be simpler to change jobs, friends or partner, than change our own behaviour. Although we can ignore our own values and thoughts for a period of time, it is not possible to keep it up forever. Eventually life becomes too destructive, unless we decide to listen and be guided by values vital to us.

Try, with an open heart, to find out which traits you are dominated by in your relationships with other people, including your strong traits as well as shadow traits. The first step towards instigating change is becoming aware of who you are. The way other people behave you will never be able to change anyway. The only thing you can do yourself, is take full responsibility for your own actions without blaming anyone else. Circumstances when you feel highly stressed or dissatisfied, are signs that time has come to instigate change and you will risk your health and well-being should you decide to ignore the signs. Either you will have to change your attitude or your situation.

In order to be able to utilise our full power we must be conscious of what, and who, we surround ourselves with, since eventually we will be drained by anyone who is not supportive or encouraging. During demanding periods in life, we may even have to close the boundaries in our closest relationships. The challenge is to understand when it is time to remain in a job, marriage, relationship or a situation that is taxing, but might teach us something. Bolting and always trying to escape tricky situations might be an indication that we are not ready to accept the consequences of our actions. Continuously complaining about the situation we are in, be it at work or in relationships, without doing anything to change the circumstances, might be a sign of being too afraid of taking responsibility for ourselves. Fear is often a stronger glue in relationships than love.

Vata imbalanced

Vata people are the most fragile and more prone to stress and pressure. They like to do the right thing and lose confidence if they end up in conflict. If their self-esteem is low, they have a tendency to take on problems other than their own, and see themselves as victims. As they like to please other people, they also have a tendency to keep changing sides. During periods of stress and excess pressure, Vata people tend to become moody, being open and easy-going one day and cross and annoyed the next. Or the insecurity might make them go quiet, pull back and become self-destructive. As soon as Vata people come off balance, they worry and become anxious. They can also become nervous and are prone to sleeping problems, as well as ambivalence and being extremely indecisive. Consequently, the agony of making decisions enhances the feeling of insecurity, which in turn can cause a lot of anguish. Frequently, they present a calm exterior despite being in turmoil internally, but when the pressure becomes too much they will have a breakdown.

Vata people have the propensity to cause chaos and insecurity in people they have relationships with, since they will constantly find something to worry about, perhaps about their health, which might be frail when they are off balance or their job, children or something else. It is not uncommon that their finances are the source of anxiety, as Vata people often find it difficult to handle money. A Vata person strives to be liked by everyone and will therefore have a hard time being true and genuine towards themselves, which might make them seem fake and dishonest to other people. The more off balance a Vata person is, the more likely they will be to disregard their own integrity and allow themselves to be influenced by other people (commonly Pitta people). A Vata person in deep despair may end up panicking and will either become indifferent and need help or become both hysterical and rebellious and accuse anyone in their vicinity.

Pitta imbalanced

The most common reason for a Pitta person becoming imbalanced is things not going their way. Their worldview is generally more rigid than the average person's, and they easily become impatient when other people do not adhere to their way of doing things, than the other constitutions. Pitta people are more resilient to stress than Vata people, whose stubbornness will make them go far beyond their limits, often at a high cost to both their physical and mental health. In relationships, they often blame their loved ones as well as other people, for their own stress and mistakes and it is not unusual for them to use their well-honed persuasive skills to manipulate others to do what they want to. Pitta people have a hot temperament which flares up in periods of excessive stress and other people will often be exposed to their anger and aggression. Should they attempt to suppress any frustration and anger, it will often be expressed as skin problems, gastritis/ulcers, cardiovascular problems or explosive headaches. Suppressing feelings is bad for everyone, but mostly for anyone with a Pitta constitution, because they have an underlying feeling that they must express what they think. The more imbalanced, the more critical and judgmental a Pitta person becomes. They will always have an opinion about everything and everybody and tend to find it difficult to accept people and situations just as they are. Pitta people assume that everyone is like them, with similar needs and wishes and will easily become controlling in relationships when they feel imbalanced. A violated Pitta person will scheme how to take revenge and regularly find it difficult to forgive other people's mistakes. They may even reach the level of becoming physically abusive to get back at the other person.

Kapha imbalance

Losing equilibrium takes some time for anyone governed by Kapha as they often choose a life involving few challenges that might induce excessive stress. The most common reason for a Kapha person to lose balance, is that they get stuck and despair about not being able to move forward. Usually they will wait until the last moment before making necessary changes, if at all, whether it be leaving a dissatisfactory job, ending a destructive relationship or starting to take care of their health, which usually entails being overweight. As a rule, Kapha people are persistent as well as strong, meaning that they are able to endure a lot. In relationships, imbalanced Kapha people become passive and unable to talk about their needs and feelings as they find it difficult to identify their feelings the more imbalanced they become. They may eventually retreat into their own shell to avoid having to interact with other people. Consequently they can be perceived as ungenerous for not giving other people access to themselves or their resources. Long-term Kapha imbalance will often be expressed in the form of obesity and deep depression with feelings of hopelessness and the person being unable to see the light at the end of the tunnel.

Balanced relationships

According to ayurvedic tradition, the unique rhythm, which stays with us throughout life, is established at birth and is called Prakriti. This translates to original rhythm. It is our Prakriti we should adhere to, if we want to strive to live a balanced, healthy and vital life. If we live a stressful life with bad eating habits and behaviours that do not benefit us, eventually we will become imbalanced and expose ourselves to various physical and mental health issues, referred to as Vikriti in Ayurveda. Becoming imbalanced is easy if we allow ourselves to follow other people's rhythms, habits and behaviours not benefitting our own constitution. The greater the difference between Prakriti and Vikriti, the deeper the imbalance will develop and it will become ever more urgent to take even better care of ourselves. The foundation for long-term well-being and staying in balance with our constitution, is to keep to our innate circadian rhythm with regard to food habits, sleep, work and exercise. Remember that the better balance we are in, the more imbalanced we can become without completely losing balance! Life will always test us with unforeseen events. Eventually we all grow old and get ill and that is when all we have got left is our good relationships. Irrespective of what we go through in life, our Prakitri, our basic constitution, remains while our personality will develop, as and when, we gain different insights which in turn will make us change values and attitude. Still, it is possible for us to live in harmony with our constitution and make sure we develop our strengths.

I have developed the Karpman's Drama Triangle further to include a few new roles we can strive for. Each constitution is prone to certain weaknesses but it is the key to discern our internal strengths which may be concealed, having never been fully utilised. By choosing a more Sattvic lifestyle we can convert the Persecutor, Rescuer and Victim and turn them into more productive and conscious character traits helping us gain strength in our relationships and become a resource for ourselves and others. Mastering being at ease in all three roles will initiate what I refer to as personal expansion, giving you access to several different aspects of yourself.

If a Persecutor with their drive and strength, becomes more Sattvic, they have the potential of mastering the role of becoming a Pathfinder. A Pathfinder is someone with great capacity to inspire others to reach common goals. Many managers have Pathfinder personalities and during the leadership courses I hold, they develop their ability to lead people by inspiring their staff to reach top results. Someone who generally assumes the role of Rescuer, helping others for selfish reasons has the potential to transforming their skills and master the role of Coach, a person who backs and supports people in achieving their own goals. Being a Coach does not always involve helping, but allowing others to try in order for them to help themselves. Anyone usually ending up in the Victim role has the opportunity to take steps towards utilising their fragility and sensitivity to develop into an inspiring Creator, someone who inspires, gets their ideas out there and initiates change and development in different ways by being bold enough to think outside the box.

Karpman's drama triangle, the roles in balance

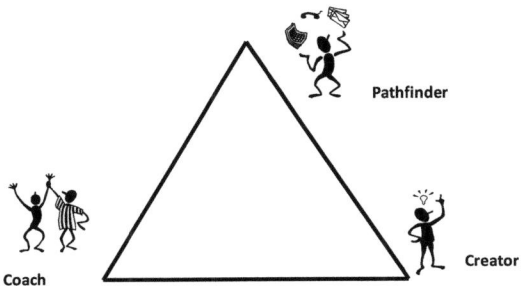

You will recognise a Pathfinder because they:

- Are passionate
- Brave enough to take command even when it is windy at the top
- Have big hearts

- Can give constructive criticism and challenge others to achieve their best
- Do not just tell you what you want to hear but what you need to hear to mature and develop
- Make things happen without bulldozing others
- Know the art of inspiring and getting people involved
- Like to share without forcing their opinions on others
- Willing to change their views as new arguments are presented
- Brave enough to stand up for what they believe in even when it is difficult
- Have the courage to apologise when they are wrong

You will recognise a Coach because they:

- Are warm hearted
- Give support when it is needed and let go when it is time
- Are emphatic
- Are understanding
- Willing to listen without judgement
- Know the art of helping others see their own light
- Guide others to achieve their goals without a hidden agenda
- Like people
- Include others
- Care

You will recognise a Creator because they:

- Are inspiring
- Dare to go their own way
- Have lots of ideas, some crazier than others
- Can see colours where others only see grey
- Dare to express their feelings
- Are flexible
- Can see things from different angles at the same time
- Are curious and try new things
- Are playful and their humour helps other people not take life too seriously

As you probably have already noticed, there is a huge difference between the less productive roles, Persecutor, Rescuer and Victim and the more energetic roles, Pathfinder, Coach and Creator. They have all kept to their basic constitutions but have changed attitude and behaviour. The difference is the latter roles no longer apply attention seeking strategies based on their ego, instead they have increasingly mastered the art of understanding, to ensure any decisions will benefit others as well as themselves. To live a balanced and harmonious life, it is inconsequential how good the food we eat is or how often we practice our yoga, if we only focus on our own well-being. There is a fine line between making sure our own needs are met, while at the same time helping others meet theirs. Sometimes we must stand our ground and fight for our own integrity and self-respect and at other times we have to let go of our own needs to keep well. Personal development from this point of view entails being able to switch between the roles rather than getting stuck in one, and by practicing alternating between the different roles you will become a more well-rounded person.

Vata in balance

Vata people in balance tend to be spontaneous and open and frequently enjoy socialising without expecting anything in return. They thrive on change as long as their foundation is solid and they very much enjoy helping other people in different circumstances. They find it easy to communicate with people they do not know and are happy to take the initiative when needed. They also speak easily and freely and are skilled at mingling and chatting about superficial things. They may be perceived as fleeting as they quickly adjust and adapt to new situations. They are creative and often come up with lots of new ideas that they have no difficulty expressing. They like to start activities but soon realise they do not have what it takes to finish the project and hand over to someone with better staying power. They are not particularly pretentious and therefore more willing to admit their failings and are open to learning new things. In relationships, Vata people are usually helpful and avoid conflict and therefore make few explicit demands. Because Vata people like to spend their money, any redecoration such as painting or buying new things for the home would probably be instigated by them. Saving for a rainy day is not high on the agenda for them and they often fritter their cash away on trips and beautiful things. Vata people see possibilities where others see restrictions. They really dislike discussing restrictions, preferring to be open and generously sharing their time and belongings. Vata people do not take life particularly seriously and know the art of living in the moment and love to enjoy themselves while they are still alive.

Pitta in balance

When Pitta people are in balance their loving energy is strong and knows no bounds, which people usually find appealing. If they have also managed to master their anger, they can be very pleasant and helpful, although they usually have an ulterior motive. People in their community, family or anyone in need can be on the receiving end of their help, but beware, there is often a reason behind their being helpful. Pitta people frequently take the initiative in different situations and have the stamina to carry things through and get involved in good causes when they are in balance. They set goals, mostly they aim high, and then they go for it. Thanks to their strong will and passion they persevere, but only as long as they believe in what they are doing. In relationships, it is the Pitta people who have the drive to make things happen to ensure they endure. They like to keep things in order and create schedules and structures for how things will work. Despite having a tendency to spot problems and risks in almost everything, they will focus on solutions and implementing necessary changes when they are in balance.

Their integrity is strong as is their instinct to protect their loved ones, although when being caring they may come across as trying to control things as well as the people close to them. They are not afraid of conflict and are inclined, or rather feel they must highlight any issues that they feel need rectifying. They would rather discuss matters of importance, ideally talking things out until the issue is cleared up. They are adventurous and love excitement, either through exhilarating leisure activities or a passionate career. Pitta people can have a stern and fairly serious outlook on life and usually plan for the future, safeguarding their future by investing any money they make, which they often do, in low and high-risk investment schemes.

Kahpa in balance

Kapha people in balance have big hearts. Since they are unpretentious, hardly anyone is scared of them. They are usually very helpful and patient and enjoy supporting and caring for other people and their property. Most people feel safe in their presence due to their natural patience and calmness. Kapha people take their time completing things and give themselves space for thinking and reflection, usually only doing one thing at a time, and moving forward methodically. When taking on a new project, a Kapha person will take the time to carefully study the pros and cons, refusing to force decisions or speed tasks along. People they meet are reassured by them due to their calm and stable demeanour.

Kapha people have stamina and keep promises. If required, they will talk, but usually sparingly and they are content being quiet even when spending time with other people. Because Kapha people are very humble they do not feel the need to change anyone making people trust them since they are so accepting. In relationships, Kapha people are loyal and helpful, and usually it is not an effort for them to look after their belongings, and if they borrow something they often return it in better shape than when they got it. As they are very accepting, Kapha people rarely instigate arguments. Due to their strong integrity they might appear aloof and do not have high expectations or preconceived ideas. They prefer meeting up with people in smaller groups, taking time nurturing close relationships. Largely, they do not feel the need to outdo themselves or convince anyone else how good they are and have mastered the art of being at peace in the here and now.

The way to balanced relationships

We all have ingrained, sometimes difficult to discern, behavioural patterns very close to our "Ego". Honestly, who am "I" and what is my personality? As mentioned previously, our constitution is something we are born with, while our personality is formed through upbringing and the environment we grow up in. We have developed certain traits, but not others, based on what type of encouragement we received from people close to us as we were growing up. To maintain enough energy and courage to nurture strong relationships, we must increasingly introduce vitality-enhancing habits in our lives. The different energies in positive relationships will be balanced evenly but frequently we end up in low-energy relationships where one part is strong and the other weak. In order to be able to remove ourselves from being involved in such destructive games, we must take on board that we have to take responsibility for expressing what it is we need to keep well. The more responsibility we are willing to take for our own well-being, without having any expectations of anyone else, the easier it will be to maintain strong and healthy relationships.

Experiencing having the rug pulled, can for some people be what is needed to stop, think and start making positive changes in life. There is not a right or a wrong. Becoming aware of our different constitutions may provide better opportunities for controlling our beliefs and consequently also how we conduct ourselves. Anyone who has learnt to fully control their thoughts and behaviour is an expert. Even if we never will become experts, at least we have the opportunity to stay on as apprentices in the School of Life.

Coaching tips

- *Describe for yourself how you relate to other people when you are in balance.*
- *Study how you relate to other people when you are stressed and uncomfortable, and start losing self-control in relation to Vata, Pitta and Kapha*
- *How would you prefer to handle your situations in relation to other people, when your needs are not met? Give as detailed a description as possible.*
- *What do you need to do to take more responsibility for your own well-being? Face the facts! Challenge yourself to look at what disturbs you without accusing either yourself or others!*
- *What skills do you need to practice more? Patience, active listening, daring to express your own opinions, relinquishing control, taking more control. Remember*

that when you find yourself in your Discomfort Zone, you are actually maturing! Once there, ensure you maintain control over how you conduct yourself.

- *What is your view of an equal, mutually respectful relationship? What do you need? How do you like it to be? What do you think the other can offer you that is lacking? In what ways can you share what you have, that is lacking for the other person?*

- *Remember that you can only change yourself and pay attention to how people you spend time with will react differently to you once you start behaving in a different way.*

9

Workforce

"Adversity is often a friend in disguise. Welcome it with gratitude, because it will bring you strength and wisdom."

Source: Unknown

Pursuing things we find meaningful, is what we were made to do. Whatever motivates us we usually want to do more of and consequently often become accomplished at. You will have noticed this if you have ever been involved in sports. Perhaps someone has brought you to the golf course for a golf lesson. If you found it exciting hitting and aiming the ball at a particular spot on the course, you have probably returned to the golf course again. You took several lessons, honed your skills and met like-minded people who inspired you to become even better. Then one day, you were on the golf course putting, exceeding your past performance and playing really well. You were in the flow, your putting was perfect, everything just clicked and the feeling of wanting to do it over and over again kept coming over you. It happens, as long as we are motivated!

Now imagine a similar scenario with respect to your work, a job that you have chosen carefully. You have been educated and have the skills within an industry to which you are suited. You can develop and utilise your skills and strengths, which allows you to continuously develop and you are driven to keep doing better and better. True? In my work in guiding management, I frequently find that the experience of far too large a proportion of staff, is that their skills and strengths are not being utilised. This is often the case in companies I am asked to support in the development of their employees. A Gallup survey conducted by the researcher Donald O. Clifton, Professor in psychology, collected data into people's skills and strengths in the last 40 years. It revealed that only one third of the 10 million people around the world included in the study about motivation in the workplace, agreed strongly that *"They have the opportunity to work with what they are best at, every day in their job"*. The study showed that people who have the opportunity to utilise their skills in their work each day, are six times more motivated in their work and their life quality was more than three times higher than those who did not agree that they utilised their skills and strengths in their work each day.

In 2005, Gallup performed a different study to establish what happens to employees whose managers focused primarily on the employee's strengths, the employee's weaknesses or ignored the employee. The results showed that the risk of employees losing motivation increased by 40% if ignored by their manager. If managers focused on employees' weaknesses the risk of employees losing motivation increased by 22%, while the risk of employees losing motivation rose by 1% in cases where the manager focused on their skills. As you can see, having a manager who ignores you, is even more demotivating than one who keeps focusing on your weaknesses. The most striking thing is, that if you are lucky enough to have a manager who is focused on your skills, it is highly likely that you also are very ambitious at work. Perhaps this is obvious to you but the question is why do organisations not concentrate on employees' strengths to a higher degree? The study shows the significant potential managers and directors have access to, tap into to enhance staff, as well as their own motivation. The most common question I receive from the managers and directors is: What has to be done to increase staff motivation? The corporate culture I usually encounter is problem-based and time is spent on problem-solving issues that need rectifying. The first question is almost always, "What is the problem?", which of course is a highly relevant question, although remaining at the problem-solving stage puts businesses at risk of not getting past the point of keeping their heads above water. Asking questions such as: What makes our team unique? What are our strengths? What are we good at? will steer the company in a completely different direction and open things up for astonishing and spectacular results.

Doctors study diseases to understand health, psychologists have studied mental illness to learn how to find contentment and at school and work too much time is devoted to identifying, analysing and changing our weaknesses in order to become stronger. Studying and focusing on faults and mistakes is necessary to a certain degree, but will not enhance the skills of staff and pupils. By deciding to focus on strengths instead, a different path will open up. If asking people what their weaknesses are, most will easily rattle off 20 of their most telling weaknesses, while asking the same group to state their 20 strongest traits would take them longer to reveal, if at all.

Why is this? The language we have been taught enables us to express faults, imperfections and weaknesses. We have adopted a mindset that arouses questions such as: What is wrong? What is not working? Such questions will never support people in developing their unique skills. Diversity, when it is encountered, is often described in negative terms, as we lack enough vocabulary to fully describe the appeal of diversity. Adopting this mindset will create a belief system that will innately censor, and discount anything we find different or unusual from what we are used to and only include that which is similar and homogenous from our own perspective. For a company this can be detrimental. A new paradigm is required to increase the flow and enhance the level of ambition in organisations, one built on people's skills and strengths. Only then will we surpass ourselves and create winning results while having fun along the way. The Gallup survey I mentioned previously, tragically shows that the longer an employee stays in an organisation and the higher up the traditional career ladder they climb, the less likely it is that they, *"Strongly agree that they use their strengths in their work each day"*. However, this also shows the enormous potential every organisation has of enhancing staff motivation and commitment. We, as the employees, would reap the benefits many times over were we encouraged to utilise our skills and strengths in our work each day. We would become healthier, feel happier, be more loyal and committed, will perform better, be more efficient and, above all, a productive corporate culture will thrive when staff are encouraged to exceed themselves. Still, how is it that we continuously focus on issues which actually create less commitment, motivation and efficiency at work?

No doubt you will remember from a previous chapter, that we all have an innate negativity filter through which we view the world. Similar to when we go through a rough patch and we privately start viewing the world through a negative filter, this also happens in companies going through development and change. The focus is mostly on finding obstacles to rectify rather than looking for and enhancing the good examples. To illustrate, we will look at sports again. Imagine that you want to be the world's number one downhill skier. Would you then consult the lowest ranking downhill skier the world has ever seen, to find out what mistakes they have made, in order for you to avoid repeating them on your way to the top? Or would you turn to the top-ranking skier in the world to establish what skills and strengths they have applied in order to be the best? Obviously, you would consult the best, anything else would be absurd. Still, this is exactly what we tend to do in our private as well as working lives. The Gallup study researchers analysed what successful managers have in common, they found that most successful managers adhere to two beliefs:

1. Each person can learn to become proficient at almost anything.
2. Each person's greatest potential for growth is concealed within their greatest weaknesses.

According to Marcus Buckingham, author of the book "*Now Discover Your Strength*", based on data from the comprehensive

Gallup survey, there are two prominent features of organisations having adopted the above beliefs.

Employee development plans are based around their ability to enhance their weaknesses.
Meetings usually start off with questions like: What is the problem? What is difficult? What needs changing? What is wrong?
To adopt a new approach based on skills and strengths, we must revise our perception of people. Below are the two most important conclusions drawn by the most successful leaders:

1. The talent of each person is consistent and unique.
2. The greatest potential for development can be found in each person's foremost strengths.

Based on the above differing results, we must first master a new way of communicating, conducting ourselves evaluating what is important, and empowering ourselves and others to discover and enhance our most unique and outstanding talents. Ask those you know who have achieved success in a certain area, what it is that makes them so successful. What do you think their reply will be? Well, that they have had and still have the opportunity to do what they are good at! Each and every single day. However, this does not mean that they are equipped with *all* skill sets needed to achieve success, all it means is that they make the best of what they have. Of course, we must not completely ignore our weaknesses, problems will arise unless we "fix" them but it is worth remembering that these areas will not be your most unique successful part of you.

People are different

Acknowledging and taking everybody's differences into account goes against the entrenched idea that everyone must be treated equally in the workplace. The later idea, however, might extinguish motivation. Comparing departments at work with a sailing team, we would soon realise that if everyone had similar skill sets, whether as captain, navigator or crew, the team would not be particularly successful. The first thing to safeguard is, that the right person is in the right place. It would be counterproductive to make a sailor navigate or vice versa. If the captain is renowned for driving the crew to success by utilising their skills and strengths on a well-equipped boat, the likelihood of highly skilled people being attracted to join the crew on the boat would increase. The captain's main task is to ensure that the right person, with the right skills, is in the right place. For instance, in light wind and calm weather the captain can hand over the helm to less skilled helmsmen in order for them to learn, as steering slightly off course then will not make much difference, while the captain's role increasingly becomes more important as the wind speed escalates. As a precaution, the captain will want to keep a closer eye on how the helmsman commands the boat in gale force, to safeguard it from going too far off course. In full storm the entire crew will look to the captain and hope that he or she has the necessary skills needed for getting through the bad weather (the crisis). However, the more skilful at positioning people with the right skills in positions where they have the opportunity to fully utilise their skills and strengths, the greater the chance of the team being really successful and finishing first. The premise for the team is, of course, that everyone will want to sail the same way, has the same goal and can communicate clearly, easily and directly with each other. In sailing strategy, you must study the boat's strength, establish in which wind it is the fastest and how it handles the sea, etc. These issues will always be considered when choosing a route. Considering the strengths and potential of the crew creates conditions for how a team can work together. Who complements who? Who can learn from each other? The culture onboard, that is, how feedback is presented, is critical for how far the team can go to outdo itself. How the team communicates is also crucial for safety and security on board, which is critical for the performance in a storm when the boat is far from land.

These basic principles for sailing success can apply also to organisations. Most of the companies I encounter in my work have understood the same importance having a visible and well-communicated vision with goals and milestones in place. The clearer we, as employees are about the vision and goals, the easier it is for us to keep to the right course in our daily work. The benefit of different corporate cultures, that is, the informal, accepted way of communicating and conducting yourself within an organisation, will generally differ. Values guiding staff on how to conduct themselves at work will generally have been articulated. Respect, empathy, teamwork and customer focus are just some of the most common values that are adopted. Although it is easy to say the words, it can be difficult to understand the full meaning of them, however since we all have our own ideas about what they stand for. So how well do we give feedback and encouragement to each other based on each other's strengths? And how do we give feedback to each other when we perceive things differently? Through the understanding that we are all different, that we have different strengths and skills, we will more easily be able to support ourselves and others in developing and using our strengths.

Within Ayurveda there is, as you already know, a deep understanding about our differences. Certainly, everyone will not become highly skilled at everything, but everyone can become seriously sharp in areas that they have natural talent and the prerequisites for. With help of the self-assessment test that follows, you can more easily understand your and others differences, similarities and strengths. With a deeper understanding about these concepts we can also be more efficient and creative to support our own as well as others strengths and talents.

Add a 1 before the statement you think best describes you. Add ½ a point each should two statements resonate equally. Add up the total of each column and write the total in the boxes below.

	Vata	**Pitta**	**Kapha**
Activity	Fast, flexible, somewhat restless, lots of balls in the air.	Effective, goal oriented, ambitious, structured.	Calm, one thing at a time, not in a hurry.
Mentality	Lots of thoughts to consider, quick & agile mind.	Sharp intellect, logical, analytical, concentrated.	Stable, calm, broad intellect, contemplative.
Learning	Learns quickly, audio memory.	Learns quickly & effectively, visual memory.	Need time for learning, practical learning (hands-on).
Memory	Forgetful.	Sharp & structured memory.	Remembers for life.
Decision making	Irresolute, see many alternatives.	Makes decisions following quick deliberation.	Requires time to make decisions, happy with decisions made.
Lifestyle	Tends to change	Mostly well organised,	Stable & regular

	direction in life, particularly regarding food & sleep. Dislikes strict routines. Easily bored.	structured daily routines, commonly tight deadlines. Delays frustrates easily. Tries to be time efficient.	routines. May find new routines difficult, prefers a comfortable lifestyle.
Stress	Easily agitated, becomes worried/anxious during times of high stress levels.	Bites the bullet and carries on, frustration and irritation that might turn into stomach/skin issues during high stress.	Takes time to become affected by stress. Becomes quiet and introverted during stressful times.
Creativity	Inquisitive, many ideas, likes to test new thoughts.	Assimilates new ideas after careful consideration.	Delays assimilating new ideas.
Finances	Likes to spend money on impulse buys.	Spends after careful consideration. Quality conscious.	Rarely impulse buys, prefers to save for the future.

Mood	Changeable.	Temperamental.	Calm & stable.
Endurance	Limited but intensive endurance.	Endurance, strong willpower.	Very stable and extended endurance
Illness inclination	Falls ill easily, intermittent pain, dry, cracked skin, sleep disturbances.	Infections, inflammation, gastritis, stomach ulcers, skin issues, migraines.	Rarely ill, more likely to develop chronic issues such as obesity, diabetes, asthma.

Total score			

Our strengths

Now that you have completed the test your profile has been revealed. As mentioned earlier, we all have our own unique combination of the three doshas Vata, Pitta and Kapha. Depending on your particular constitution, inherently you will have different strengths and skills. Some you might have developed and use daily in your life, while others are yet to emerge since encouragement and response from our friends and family are needed to develop them. Actively developing our skills creates enormous power which can help us reach far past our imagined limits. Consciously focusing on developing your strengths and skills will help you invite more of that which creates success for you and reject that which merely keeps your head above the parapet.

Let us take a look at different strengths, based on which constitution we have. Our best chance of developing what we are really good at, is when we are balanced. Therefore, it is key to ensure your private life is also well balanced. Unless work and private life are balanced, nobody will be successful in the long run.

Vata

Vata people, as a rule, like to be among people. They really like to provide service and sort things out for others. They are service-minded and spontaneous and easily make contact with other people. In safe and supporting environments they are full of ideas, very creative and good at initiating new projects. They are very flexible and have the ability to take on board new perspectives. They are agile both in body and mind and quickly get new things off the ground. They are inherently curious which leads them to dare to try new things. When in balance, Vata people can tap into their sensitivity and imagination, which is often expressed in artistic contexts such as music, art, literature, etc. Vata people are quick both in words and action. Their natural openness makes others feel welcome and appreciated and it is common for people dominated by Vata to choose work which requires a lot of contact with other people. In order to stay motivated, committed and on task, Vata people generally need clarity about any assignments and goals.

Since they are more fragile than the other constitutions and more sensitive to stress and criticism, Vata people need good support.

Vata people are often found in customer service, receptions and other service jobs which demand flexibility and adaptability. My experience is that people dominated by Vata are able to do a lot for others, but it is also important to fit in time to recover, or else they will easily end up out of balance and overwhelmed. They usually value not having to take sole responsibility which can feel far too challenging. It is easy for Vata people to be creative and innovative since they do not feel the need to control everything, hence a lot of people in creative work are strongly dominated by Vata. Usually, Vata people like to keep many balls in the air simultaneously, which puts them at risk of ending up in too much chaos, which can make them deflate. Most Vata people are unpretentious and find it easy to admit they do not know how to do something but are quick learners.

Vata people communicate freely and easily with most people they encounter and they are prone to being pro rather than against. When they meet complex people, they often have the ability to help them become more positive, because of their friendly attitude. Their primary gifts are flexibility, adaptability, social skills, creativity, thinking outside conventional constructs and agility. Vata energy in balance, creates ease, flow and a feeling of boundlessness.

Pitta

Pitta people are strong individuals who have a great ability to set themselves goals and then go for them. When they are in balance they are passionate and warm-hearted with an immense capacity to motivate and inspire others to help them develop and outdo themselves. They find it easy to structure themselves and implement ideas. They are analytical, weigh things up and look at situations critically before getting involved. They easily apply themselves, are good at managing others, find great pleasure in challenging projects and have the capacity to inspire and give others the courage to try. They take control spontaneously and are conscious of quality. They tap into their strong willpower to implement their ideas which other people think are just about impossible, hence they are often a great inspiration for people around them. In balance, Pitta people can utilise their full potential to become great leaders and people who make a difference for many. Their morals are strong and their decisions are well balanced and ethical. They rarely leave anything by chance since they want the power to realise their ideas. They enjoy voicing and discussing their opinions. Anyone dominated by Pitta often seeks positions in which they can influence and be in control. Managers, doctors, politicians, high-ranking officers and teachers are some examples of professions primarily dominated by people with Pitta energy.

Pitta people in balance are good speakers. They communicate powerfully and intensely and usually in a captivating and inspiring way. They have the capacity to challenge others with their strong and dominant personality and may be the ones having the courage to stand up for important values. The primary gifts of Pitta people are staying focused with a great ability to analyse, evaluate and put theory into practice. In balance, Pitta energy emits strength, passion, determination and courage to dare to believe in whatever they have resolved to do.

Kapha

Kapha people easily create stability and security. They are very emphatic and have the ability to listen without being judgmental. They are calm and loyal, and can tap into their endurance power when others give up. They have the strength to care for others and have no difficulty in working away methodically on their own. They enjoy their own company and carry on even in the darkest of times. They are methodical and when they start a project they complete it carefully, as they let things take the time that is required for carrying the projects out properly. Given the space to reflect, their capacity to look at things from a birds-eye perspective is greater than for the other constitutions and they also have the ability to help others see things from a long-term perspective. When Kapha people are living to their full potential they are strong, persevering and hugely caring, and can instil hope and confidence in others. To a greater extent than others, Kapha people go into more methodical, long-term professions which require them to be very thorough. Accountants, auditors, care-givers and craftsmen represent occupations often prevailed by Kapha energy. Kapha people generally avoid being in situations involving too much stress. They often stick to the decisions they have made and prefer long-term conditions and therefore desire change less than the other doshas.

Kapha people's strength lies in being able to listen when other people speak, and they also take the time to reflect on what the other person is saying. At work, Kapha people emit humility, perseverance and stability.

The strengths of the different constitutions

Vata	Pitta	Kapha
Flexible	Focused	Calm
Moving intellect	Analytical	Emphatic
Full of ideas	Directing	Listener
Creative	Implementing	Takes one thing at a time
Spontaneous	Controlling	Reflecting
Good at initiating projects	Evaluating	Methodical
Service minded	Engaging	Long-term perspective
Uses many words	Speaks clearly and directly	Use fewer words
Wishes to be loved	Likes setting goals and completing them	Likes caring for others

Utilising and developing our strengths

In order to develop, we need to take on the challenge of considering our behaviour and attitudes as well as other people's perception of us. Success, as mentioned earlier, is when you have reached a point of being able to create the outcomes you would like. The most prized skills in the working environment have become social skills, which will increase in importance as communication techniques are refined.

If you are serious about fighting for your strengths and developing your skills, you must have the courage to step outside your comfort zone where you feel secure. As we get older our curiosity in trying new things diminishes and we prefer to stay in our comfort zone. We die a little as we become less and less curious. Trying out a new way of thinking each day is a way to challenge ourselves and our habits. It is time to call on the powers we possess for making a difference in the world. Never before have innovative thinking and creativity been in such high demand to solve the huge challenges we are being subjected to. We have the choice of regarding the issues as frightening or as challenging possibilities for creating a whole new outlook on how humanity can exist side by side. The more chaos, that is Vata, the more we need the stability, perseverance and care of Kapha..

Start paying attention to what comes particularly easy for you in your daily work, where your strengths are, and try to minimise your weaknesses, to avoid them standing in your way. Enhance your awareness of what it is that gives you energy, what you really like to do. It is in this area that you have the potential for creating real success. Take on board that without a doubt, you have not yet developed all of your potential skills and strengths. By challenging yourself to do new things, or old things in a new way, you have the potential to discover more about yourself and your strengths. It is also worthwhile considering who gives and who drains you of energy, amongst the people you surround yourself with. To consciously choose more and more of what you are good at, is a safe way to ensure you develop and improve, whether it is being a parent, an athlete, a manager, employee, author, carpenter, grandfather or whatever it is that you want to be really successful at.

The biggest stumbling block for our own success is ourselves. Many people balk at quitting a permanent job in order to have the courage to go for their dream, but giving yourself the opportunity to go for your dreams, makes life grand and beautiful! It is better to die knowing that we have lived fully every day and given our dreams life, than to discover that we just stayed in our comfort zone throughout our life. Many of the people I coach balance between realising their dreams and sticking with something that is not meaningful to them, but feel safe. One thing that has become clear to me, the more people I meet and coach, is that we have a lot more to give when we have the confidence to follow both our heart and our brain, in order to achieve our deepest dreams. To those around you, following your dreams may seem odd and strange as well as challenging. So be it, the worst thing that can happen when going for your dreams is that you might fail, which is the best practice for becoming successful. Learn to fail, dust yourself off and get up again. Perseverance is one of the primary characteristics that successful people possess.

Developing Vata

Utilise your learning skills to see what you can learn about security and balance, but make sure you have the courage to stop and reflect. Doing that will ensure your swiftness and agility also gives you focus and integrity to help you persevere for longer, which will create a more stable environment for those around you. Your swiftness, which is also expressed in the many words you use and the quick speed at which you communicate, can be honed by practicing considering what it is you really would like to say and why. Practice speaking briefly and clearly. Make sure you are prepared before meetings and conversations by thinking through in advance what it is you really want to get across. To stay strong, Vata people can utilise set routines at work, to avoid the tendency to drift off and loose track. Keep to routines and structures to create a basic framework that will allow yourself to be spontaneous and creative. Beware of working too much, although having a lot to do once in a while is not a problem if during stressful times you make sure to compensate with Vata-balancing activities.

To utilise your full potential you must safeguard getting the sleep you need. Sleep disorders signal that you might have taken on too much. Eat regularly and during the winter months, eat warm food and drink boiled warm water regularly. Meditation is one of the most powerful ways of quickly winding down (please refer to the meditation at the end of this book for instructions). When you have become used to meditating, you can simply find a peaceful place to meditate in all sorts of situations; on the plane, on the bus, in the office or any other place where you can sit peacefully for 10 to 20 minutes.

Developing Pitta

As a Pitta person, you will always make sure that your calendar is fully booked, often resulting in you running behind schedule. You enjoy being on the move which makes you feel motivated and involved. You have the skill to quickly analyse and prioritise which decisions must be made and then go from theory to practice. Should you end up in a stressful and pressured situation, you run the risk of creating more friction, becoming dominant and closing the door to open dialogue, due to the way you communicate. You may become cynical, your fuse might be short and you may take your bad temper out on anyone nearby. To return to being strong, you must cool yourself down immediately and it is advisable to take some time out to create some distance with the problem. By pausing and trying to involve those who you depend on and have around you, you will increase the influence you have over the situation and get them more excited about whatever it is you want to accomplish. Practice asking others what they think and make sure you listen actively, with interest and empathy.

Make sure to take NPR-time off regularly, that is, No Particular Reason, which would be a challenge since usually you would want to max your time. Working overtime for extended periods of time will put you at risk of creating a blazing fire internally.

Compensating by exercising intensely will only add to the problem. If the fire rages too intensely and you end up with skin problems, gastritis or haemorrhaging, it is time to ask yourself how your needs are being met in your working life. Start by taking control of your working hours and make sure you eat at the same time each day. Establish a regular bed time at 11 pm at the latest since you have a tendency to get a second wind between 11 pm and 1 am at night, which is destructive. Learning to set time aside to enjoy just being, is the most important skill you can master to achieve balance and learn to develop your strengths. Practice, with emphasis on balance not intensity, if you are prone to Pitta imbalance.

Developing Kapha

If you are dominated by Kapha, you will usually be deeply knowledgeable within your field. You have the capacity to complete your tasks thoroughly and with determination. You are reliable and would never contemplate dropping a project before it is done. Deadlines are not your thing, instead you want to be able to complete your assignments and tasks based on the time it takes, which means that you do not make rash decisions. Your strength is to be able to stand your ground without creating discord and your communication style makes others feel actively involved. You are unpretentious and do not need to be the centre of attention. When you begin to whine about everything and everyone, your general dissatisfaction with everything often stems from a feeling of being incapable of changing your situation, because you do not know where to begin. That is when it is time to tap into all the courage you have to start implementing change. To remain strong, you must always make sure you keep to regular activities to safeguard you, feeling involved in any change that affects you. Should you also begin to gain weight due to a too comfortable, but not healthy, lifestyle, you will have adopted a lifestyle that will alienate you even further from your strengths. Make sure you exercise regularly, eat less and do not forget to remain curious. Practice stepping out of your comfort zone and do something new that you do not usually do. Make conversation spontaneously with people you would not normally talk to. Join in an activity you otherwise would not have tried. Set time-limited goals for your activities and keep to them. Exercise is key for you in order to remain strong permanently, ideally daily but at least three times per week.

The workplace based on Vata, Pitta and Kapha

Let us look at different workplaces through a Vata, Pitta and Kapha filter. Since the three qualities exists in everything, we can also define workplaces by the three doshas, based on how they operate. We will consider a few different types. Healthcare, for example, is a workplace focused on care and looking after people. It is dominated by Kapha energy. Looking closer at different parts of the healthcare system it becomes apparent that those who carry out and analyse tests, are more dominated by Pitta energy, including accuracy, precision and control, traits important for the job. Pre-school and nursery staff who look after small children are usually dominated by Kapha, with focus on care and security, while the person taking on the management is generally dominated by Pitta. Dance, theatre and music are dominated by Vata, with Pitta being a strong element, whereby the creative process is characterised by chaos as well as perfectionism. The more creativity, the more Vata. Dancers are dominated by Vata's lightness and flexibility, while advertising agencies are dominated by Vata because they are dependent on the creative process and being able to brainstorm freely. Necessary creativity is easily disturbed by too hard and fast rules. Schools are dominated by people who want to teach, being foremost a Pitta energy, although many teachers also have Kapha energy, especially if they teach younger children. University lecturers are usually governed more by Pitta, particularly if they are also involved in research. Just identifying different workplaces this way will not solve anything, but it can give an insight into whether or not you are in an environment that would stimulate you to develop. With an understanding of the different energies Vata, Pitta and Kapha together with Sattva, Rajas and Tamas, we can evaluate different workplaces, teams and individuals to discern what is going on and what must evolve in order to enhance power and creativity.

A lot around us moves faster and faster. Transmission of information via the internet and all the new manners of communicating finds us in a constant stream of information. We are subjected to higher demands and being less able to limit ourselves as to what we really want to and can handle receiving. The focus is predominantly on performance, and increasingly jobs are performance-oriented. I believe that Kapha energy will be needed to a greater extent to maintain balance. Effectively, this means that the more flexible we have to be in our daily lives, the more important it will be to take time out regularly to prevent becoming too overwhelmed due to an overload of impressions. According to research, on the other hand, it has been proven that youths around age 20 are more intelligent and able to handle more impressions in a short time, without experiencing it stressful. Humans are changeable and flexible and will hopefully find smarter ways to balance our day to day lives.

Coaching tips

- *Write down 5 of your foremost strengths (attributes) that you utilise in your everyday life.*
- *Write down in which situations you have felt/feel flow and work satisfaction.*
- *What would you like to work with, how would you like to work and in which context would you like to work? Describe in much detail as possible and keep your strengths in mind while doing this.*
- *What would you like your working life to be like in 1 year?*
- *What would you like to have in your working life in 5 years?*
- *What are the 5 predominant changes you must implement to come closer to your goal?*
- *Write down your milestones and design a timeline for when you will have achieved them.*
- *Take action! It is only when we start doing in real life that change becomes possible.*

10

Give vitality a chance

"The whole world is a series of miracles, but we're so used to them we call them ordinary things".

H.C. Andersen

What is it that gives us power, happiness and harmony throughout a long life? If you already know the answer you can count yourself lucky. Too many of us are still searching, despite at times believing we have found it; through a new therapy, a new kitchen, a career or having more money in the bank. All and any of this can be part of the journey towards the goal, although to my mind, we are still blind to what we really long for. Going back to the Trobriands, the islands in the South Pacific where people have lived almost disease-free for thousands of years, in peace with themselves and those around them, we can reflect on what the answer to the riddle of happiness and satisfaction is. Is there even just one answer? Maybe there are several? Clearly, we have not found it in our culture where we consume huge amounts of medicine to ease physical, mental and existential symptoms. We do not live in a sustainable society since the majority of people still live below the poverty line, but still we continue to be under the delusion that the resources we tap into are infinite. We know that an economy continually dependent on steadily increasing consumption is doomed to collapse. If it also brings short-term gains contributing to the environment being destroyed for many future generations, or our oceans becoming depleted of fish, then we must realise that it is time to adopt a new paradigm. As always, change begins with a thought, first embraced by few, and eventually by more and more people until it is endorsed by the majority. This is where we are now. Ravi Batra, Professor in Economy, originally from India but working in the USA, describes the necessity of a shift that needs to happen on all levels, particularly on a global economy level where a growing number of people have experienced what short-term thinking can lead to.

How is this linked with our life force, then? I really believe that world peace always begins with peace in our own heart. If we do not feel good, are not involved in healthy and close relationships, not living a life in balance, it is difficult to see how we will be able to create the necessary changes that are sorely needed now. A growing number of people desire meaningfulness in their lives including a job that they enjoy, an evolving relationship, integrity and opportunities for development. We are beginning to take on board that our own life choices affect other people too. A tendency towards increased concern about the cultivation and production of the food we eat is gaining momentum, not only with regard to our own wellbeing but the realisation that repercussions will ensue if we do not help and support those growing the food. We would not have any fish to eat, should the fishermen deplete the fish stock and if the tomato grower's health deteriorates due to spraying toxic chemicals on the tomatoes we will eat, that would also present problems for us. What is involved in entering into a new way of thinking? We can refer to it as a paradigm shift, since the scope of the changes required to create sustainable development is immense. Turbulence, uncertainty and instability will always accompany any extensive period of transition, which effectively means we enter Vata time, with short-term thinking, turbulence and insecurity. During times of unrest we frantically search for order, morality and deeper meaning in life. Ravi Batra has described these cycles in society in the book *The Great Depression of 1990.* He explains that it is impossible to halt a development process and that in difficult and turbulent times we look for the answer to the question "why?". He also describes that a leader able to formulate answers, is also the one who can impel the authority to lead. We need brave, innovatively thinking leaders more than ever.

We need a world where access to a good life is natural. Where resources we use are on the same level as can be renewed. Where happiness and well-being revolve around affirming and tapping into our strengths, not only for our own gain but also for our fellow human beings, as well as future generations. Where companies view local and global accountability as a natural part of their activities. Where those of us who are employed by these companies become involved to reach the best outcome, both locally and globally. A world in which we take on board that if we want to live a powerful and balanced life, we need to stop covering up our symptoms, and instead realise that we have all the strengths and talents that is needed for change for the better.

Dialogue

David Bohm, a world leading Professor in theoretical physics who died in 1992, realised the value of meeting and communicating to build bridges. Amongst other things he has said; "To communicate is to make something common", and in his book "Dialogue" he describes a method for non-judgmental communication. The word dialogue comes from the Greek word *dia* – through, and *logos* – words, which signify putting your thoughts into words. The point of Bohm's dialogue is that a group of people together freely express their own, and take on board the thoughts of the other members of the group without passing judgement. This is in contrast to discussion, arguments or even worse, agitation, which would be more concerned with division and creating differences. A dialogue does not have any winners nor any losers, it just is. Bohm implied that if people who are dependent on each other in different ways are left to express their thoughts without being judged, the potential for new perspectives and solutions will increase. Bohm's method of dialogue has been adopted by various organisations and in different circumstances where finding new solutions have been required. It may sound simple, but the energy created when people come together like this is very powerful and life-affirming.

For instance, a Bohm dialogue was conducted during the abolishment of apartheid in South Africa, since those involved realised the importance of all different parties being able to communicate with each other, and that this was prerequisite for a lasting agreement. White ex-police officers who had violently abused Coloured people were brought together in a room with

Coloured people who had been subjected to the brutal violence, as well as politicians and people from different organisations. Essentially, this dialogue process facilitated almost inconceivable compassion brought on by the different perspectives of those involved. Understandably, in these circumstances a lot of different feelings arose that could now be expressed in words. Another example involves a multinational company that gathered different departments dependent on each other to produce products, as they needed to adopt a new way of thinking in order to cooperate and develop products. No individual person had a solution, therefore the employees were put into different circles where completely new, innovative solutions nobody had thought of before were conceived.

The purpose of a dialogue circle is not to analyse things, win an argument or exchange opinions, rather it is more about listening and letting go of thoughts to make room for totally different perspectives. We do not need to agree or take a stance, all we need to do in these dialogues is to listen to everyone's ideas and thoughts. It is a unique tool for bringing opposing groups, requiring a new structure, together. Bohm's dialogue is based on ancient traditions which have been used by all different cultures, whereby people have gathered in circles and listened to each other until ready to make a decision. The female elders in one native American tribe in the USA were positioned on the periphery of the circle and decisions were not made until their opinions had been voiced, as it was acknowledged that their ability to see to the greater good for humanity and future generations was better. Perhaps unusual for some, this type of dialogue meetings eliminate hierarchy or someone attempting to get into a higher position with. The prerequisite being that participants are willing to let go of any potential roles during the dialogue. The perception of many participants of what actually happens, is that the dialogue is very rewarding and that they have had a genuine meeting with other people.

Intimate and close relationships

After many years working with people both professionally and with their personal development, I am convinced that the primary source of lasting joy and harmony is our ability to be fully present when meeting other people. Having the confidence to be true to your deepest values when you are with someone else, letting your guard down and putting yourself at risk of being let down and disappointed, is the hardest but also the most rewarding experience you can have. Many of us share the longing for close and intimate relationships, although most of us do not know how to be close and intimate with others.

We tend to compartmentalise our relationships with colleagues, relatives, friends, family, acquaintances, etc. Trying to find a place in life where you can be close to others without wondering whether you will be accepted or not, is most likely the reason many personal development courses fill up quickly these days. We need to find breathing space in our daily lives to just be, without needing to achieve anything. As long as we believe we have something to lose if we show our true self, it will be difficult to feel closeness and connected. Loneliness wears many people down as we do not really know how to bond with other people to create loving relationships. An up and coming movement to facilitate these types of meetings is called "Sharing", which in many ways is reminiscent of Bohm's method of dialogue. Once or twice per month, meeting up with 6 to 10 people to share your own thoughts without being interrupted or judged, is rewarding for many people. A Sharing group can be formed spontaneously with people you know, or a group can be formed between people looking for new ideas or to feel they belong somewhere.

Give success a chance

Let us be inspired by the following quote by Marianne Williamson, "*Our deepest fear is not that we are inadequate. Our deepest fear is that we are powerful beyond measure.*" Generally, we are completely unprepared for how those around us will perceive us should we dare to show our talents, strengths and full potential and it is not uncommon for those close to us simply being unused to handling human success. It is far too easy to view things through a negative filter when looking at ourselves and those around us and think, "Who do you think you are?" or, "What makes you think that you can do something better than someone else?" Do not get caught in this trap. It is usually a trap we have carried with us since childhood and feeling helpless will not bring anything apart from making us miserable. Take a leap in life and say that you can, say that I can, say that we can, and help develop a language to highlight our strengths rather than our weaknesses. A language that helps people develop their potential so that they can achieve their dreams in life. Happy people build bridges to other people. Happy people do not start wars, instead they choose to create dialogue. If you want to create peace and harmony in the world, begin with yourself. Set an example for your children, friends and for those around you.

Happiness and harmony will come once we are ready to be happy. Most of us believe that happiness must come first, so that we have a reason to be happy. We wait and wait and wonder why happiness never comes. Start now! Help yourself to the things that are already present in your life, that you after all can be happy about. It is fully possible to be happy, despite all the things you think need changing before you can say that you are truly happy. We are far too programmed to focus on that which holds us back.

Imagine a big Great Dane that was taught as a puppy to not jump over a 50 cm high fence. As an adult it can simply step over the fence, but it has been programmed that it cannot, so it stays put inside the fence. Think about what your internal "fence" is, that holds you back from simply taking a step over to the other side, where your dreams can be realised. Time for blaming others for teaching us to stay inside the fence is running out. We cannot afford to waste our energy thinking too much about why others did not give us all the perfect conditions that we needed. It might even be an integral part of life to learn to "step over the fence" and perhaps it may also be necessary to learn that life is sometimes complicated, hard, painful and lonely. If those components were missing, how would we know which direction we need to move in, to find the greatest treasure of all, namely love for ourselves?

There is a beautiful story about a monk who went to the great Buddha and asked where to hide happiness so that the people would not be able to find it. Buddha said, "Put it in the ocean since they will not look for it there. No, they will most certainly look for it there, thought the monk. Put it deep inside the forest then. They will not go there. No, that would not work either, people will look there too. Well…I have worked it out now, said the monk: we will hide happiness deep inside their own hearts, where they will never look".

Most likely, that is how it is. We carry happiness with us every day, it is always close at hand without us knowing, we just have to become aware of it.

From Marianne Williamson's book "A Return to Love"

Our deepest fear is not that we are inadequate.

Our deepest fear is that we are powerful beyond measure.

It is our light, not our darkness that most frightens us.

We ask ourselves, Who am I to be brilliant, gorgeous, talented, fabulous?

Actually, who are you not to be?

You are a child of God.

Your playing small does not serve the world.

There is nothing enlightened about shrinking so that other people won't feel insecure around you.

We are all meant to shine, as children do.

We were born to make manifest of the glory of God that is within us.

It's not just in some of us; it's in everyone.

And as we let our own light shine, we unconsciously give other people permission to do the same!

As we are liberated from our own fear, our presence automatically liberates others!

———————————

Appendix I

Oil massage

Oil massage is an excellent way to balance Vata. Since all of us tend to have Vata in excess, depending on how we live, Vata and Pitta people will feel especially good rubbing themselves with oil in the morning after a shower.

The skin contains thousands of small nerves connecting every cell in the body. The skin is also one of the biggest producers of "peace and calm" hormones.

In pure scientific terms, oil massage works by affecting and calming the body's two governing systems; the nervous system and the endocrine system. According to ayurvedic tradition, massage rejuvenates the skin, helping our muscles relax and release Ama (toxins) from the body.

The good effects of massage:

- improves blood and lymphatic circulation
- releases and transports toxins
- reduces tiredness
- improves digestion and the immune system (through the hormonal system)
- improves sleep
- enhances our body awareness

Sesame oil should "mature" before use, that is, be heated to about 110°. You can simply check the temperature by letting a drop of water into the oil when you heat the oil. When the drop sizzles and pops up to the surface, the oil is warm enough. NB: Never leave oil on the stove unsupervised. It can catch fire.

Whole body massage (5 – 10 min)

- Start by massaging the face and ears which are important parts of massage. On the outsides of the ears there are pressure points for the whole back, in particular. The temples and behind the ears are especially good for balancing Vata. Avoid getting oil in the eyes.
- Massage the neck, throat and shoulders.
- Continue to massage down the arms applying lengthwise strokes, with circular movements over the joints. Massage each finger independently. Soft circular movements over the chest, stomach and abdomen, clockwise is usually recommended in Ayurveda since the intestines move clockwise, over the breast bone up and down.
- Massage the back, particularly the lower back, as far as you can reach.
- The legs are massaged with powerful lengthwise movements, like the arms, with circular movements over the joints.
- You can massage the soles of the feel powerfully and move your fingers around each toe.

If you have time, give yourself a nice head massage by rubbing pure sesame oil onto the whole head. Leave the oil in the hair for a while, or even better, sleep with it over the night to give it a rewarding hair mask before you wash it out.

Appendix II

Summary of the ayurvedic daily routines

Morning routines:

- Ideally, get up before Vata time is over (6:00 to 7:00).
- Drink 1-1½ cups of boiled water to get the bowels moving in the morning.
- When you brush your teeth, make sure to also scrape your tongue to remove the coating, use your toothbrush or a tongue-scraper. The tongue is an extension of your internal organs. The tongue has pressure points which are stimulated by touch.
- Have a warm shower. To shower before yoga and meditation wakes the body up and cleans our senses while the warmth softens the body. If you have a lot of Pitta, you can finish off with a cold shower.
- Massage the whole body with sesame oil or specific Vata, Pitta or Kapha oil. Massaging using sesame oil stimulates the skin as it contains thousands of small nerve fibres and is rich in hormones which affect the hormonal system. Oil massage is particularly beneficial for Vata and Pitta. For Kapha, dry massage with a sponge or glove is more beneficial.
- Do a simple relaxation programme adapted to you; for example, simple yoga, qi gong movements or something similar that you have learnt. Yoga has some simple exercises such as the sun greeting and pranayama breathing. End by going through your vision and finish with a meditation.

- Eat breakfast *according to your personal constitution* in peace and quiet. Light a candle and experience the day dawning. Now you are ready to meet a new day with all its possibilities and challenges.

More routines during the day

- Drink boiled warm water, approx. 6-8 cups in gulps, regularly during the day.
- NB: Adapt the temperature to the season and your constitution: if you are cold, drink warm, if you are warm, drink cooler.
- NB: Never blend boiled water with water from the tap!

- Pay attention to your hunger signals and eat only when hungry. Maximum 3 meals, for Vata possibly a snack in the afternoon. Do not eat between meals.
- Chew your food well to break the food down, adjust the temperature and blend the food with saliva and digestive enzymes. The digestive process will initiate signals being sent to the gastrointestinal system that food is on the way. It will also slow down mealtimes, meaning that you will perceive when you are full naturally, as well as enhancing the flavours.

Appendix III

Meditation

I recommend that you make meditation an integral part of your morning routine, because it has an overall effect internally and on our power to heal. Meditating regularly means that you help your immune system maintain its strength. You give yourself an opportunity for being still, where you can discover an internal space in which you can just be.

Meditating is not strange or hocus pocus. It means that you relax and sit comfortably in a chair or with your legs crossed, so that you are comfortable. Meditation does not involve any directions, nothing you need to achieve and, therefore, nothing that is good or bad. It just is. While meditating you can start focussing on your breathing and tell yourself to just relax and let go of any thoughts. You decide how long you will stay. The recommended time is between 10 and 20 minutes. If you have less time, then sit for 5 minutes, which is better than nothing. After a few deep breaths, start repeating AUM quietly to yourself. It does not matter how you say the mantra. When you discover that your thoughts have wandered to something else, such as work, the children, what you should buy for dinner, etc, let go of that thought and return to repeating your AUM mantra.

To explain meditation I usually use a metaphor, likening meditation to sitting in a shop window, where your thoughts come and go, thoughts being represented by the people walking by outside. Getting stuck in a thought is similar to you having jumped out of the window and followed one of the people representing that thought. Every time you notice that you are processing a thought, just let it go and jump back behind the window.

Meditation is also like diving into your internal subconscious ocean. When we delve into our internal space, we pass many thought bubbles that we easily get stuck on, which makes us return to the surface and become conscious of what we are thinking. The mantra you say quietly to yourself works as a weight belt that helps you sink inside yourself. By practicing letting go of your thoughts once you become conscious of them, you can improve your relaxation and your body will begin to experience glimpses of being mastered from inside and being completely disconnected from your wants, which would otherwise direct you day in and day out.

Meditation summary:

- Sit comfortably in a chair or on the floor (on the train, on the bus, on the plane, on a bench…).
- Close your eyes.
- Inhale deeply three times at the same time as you relax your whole body.
- Relax your jaws.
- Lay your hands, opened, on your lap.
- Repeat your mantra throughout the whole meditation.
- Every time you detect a thought, let it go and continue repeating your mantra quietly internally.
- Finish by taking a deep breath.
- Open your eyes.

Bibliography

Bohm. D. (1999). *On Dialogue.*

Douillard. J. (2001). Body, *Mind and Sport. The Mind-Body Guide to Lifelong Health, Fitness and Your Personal best.*

Maslach. C. & Leiter. M.P. (1999). *The truth about burnout: How organizations cause personal stress and what to do about it.*

Trobe. T. (2003). *Stepping out of Fear. Breaking Free of Pain and Suffering.*

Parikh. J. (1992). *Managing your Self.*

Heart. B. & Larkin. M. (1999). *Wind is my mother*

Jonsson. S. & Hagström. A. (1990). *En bro över mörka vatten.*

Frawley. D. (1992). *Ayurvedic healing. A comprehensive guide.*

Chopra. D. (1996). *Perfect health. The first practical guide to harnessing the healing power of the mind.*

Stigson. M. (1998). *Skapa din egen hälsa med Ayurveda. Insikter för livet.*

Dalai Lama & Cutler. H. (1999). *The art of happiness: a handbook for living.*

Ventegodt. S. (1998). *Quality of life. To conquer the meaning of life.*

Jeffers. S. (2001). *Feel the fear and do it anyway.*

Chopra. D. (1996). *Livets vetenskap. Vid läkarvetenskapens gränser.*

Buckingham. M. (2005). *Now discover your strengths. How to develop your talents and those of the people you manage.*

Chopra. D. (1996). *The seven spiritual laws of success.*

Antonovsky. A. (2002). *Unravelling the mystery of health*

Burenhult. G. (2004). *The perfect human.*

Levi. L. (1990). *Stress och Hälsa.* Stockholm: Karolinska Institutet för stressforskning.

Sävstam. Malin. (2008). *När livet stannar: En berättelse om att överleva*

Rath. T. (2007). *Strengthsfinder 2.0.*

Robbins. A. (2008). *Your unlimited power. Unleash your inner strength.*

Williamson, M. (2005). *A Return to Love.*